The Complete Book of
BOOKBINDING

Josep Cambras

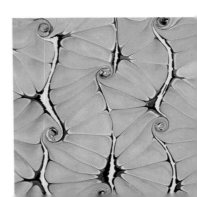

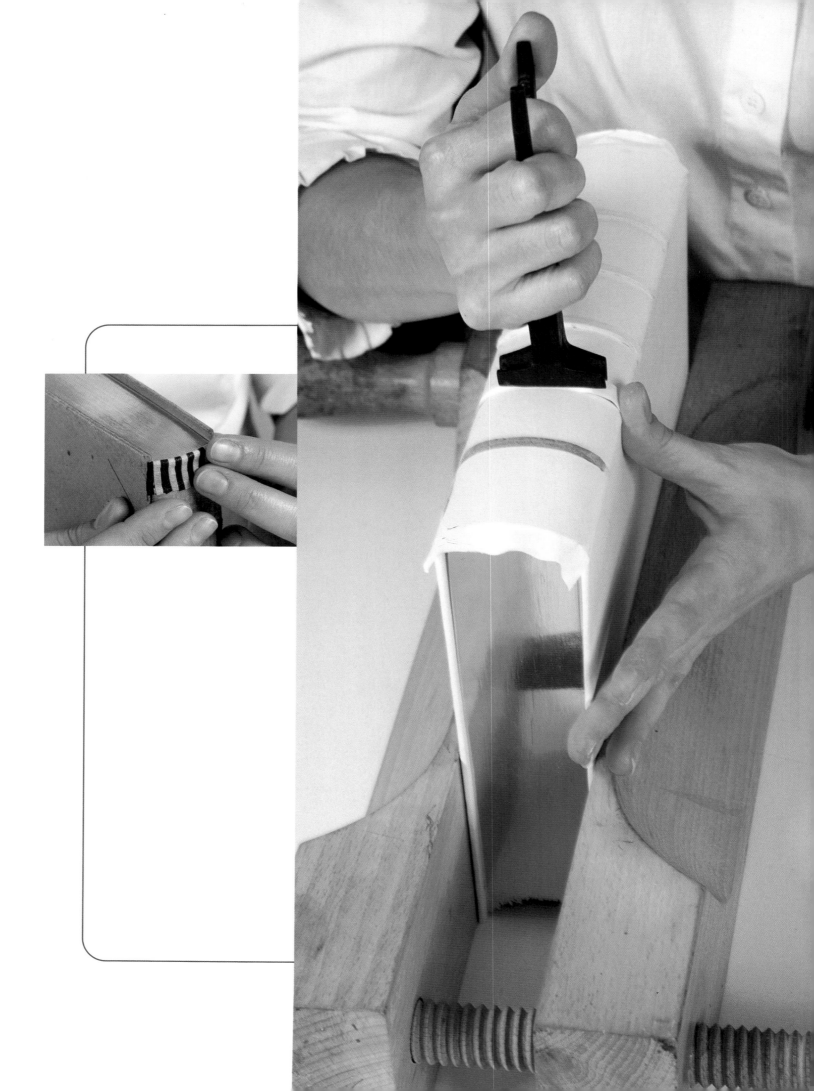

The Complete Book of
BOOKBINDING

LARK BOOKS

A Division of Sterling Publishing Co., Inc.
New York

Library of Congress Cataloging-in-Publication Data

Cambras, Josep.
  [Encuadernación. English]
  The complete book of bookbinding / by Josep Cambras.
     p. cm.
  Includes bibliographical references and index.
  ISBN 1-57990-646-X
  1. Bookbinding. I. Title.
Z271.C26 2005
686.3–dc22
                              2004014484
First Edition

Published by Lark Books, A Division of
Sterling Publishing Co., Inc.
387 Park Avenue South, New York, N.Y. 10016

© 2004, Josep Cambras

Distributed in Canada by Sterling Publishing,
c/o Canadian Manda Group, One Atlantic Ave., Suite 105
Toronto, Ontario, Canada M6K 3E7

Distributed in the U.K. by Guild of Master Craftsman Publica-
tions Ltd.,
Castle Place, 166 High Street, Lewes, East Sussex, England
BN7 1XU
Tel: (+ 44) 1273 477374, Fax: (+ 44) 1273 478606, Email:
pubs@thegmcgroup.com, Web: www.gmcpublications.com

Distributed in Australia by Capricorn Link (Australia) Pty Ltd.,
P.O. Box 704, Windsor, NSW 2756 Australia

If you have questions or comments about this book,
please contact:
Lark Books
67 Broadway
Asheville, NC 28801
(828) 253-0467

Manufactured in China
All rights reserved
ISBN: 1-157990-646-X

Editorial Director:
Lluís Borràs
Editorial Assistant and Picture File:
Cristina Vilella
Text and Technical Coordination:
Josep Cambras
Text of the History of Bookbinding:
Ramon Serra
Text of Tools and Materials:
Pilar Estrada
Dust Jacket:
Montse Buxó
Collection Design:
Josep Guasch
Layout and Pagination:
Estudi Guasch, S. L.
Photography:
Jordi Vidal
Illustrations:
Jaume Farrés
Translated from the Spanish by:
Eric A. Bye, M.A.
English Edition Technical Editor:
Scott Keller

1st Edition: October, 2003
© Parramón Publishing, Inc. 2003
08010 Barcelona, Spain
A Division of Norma Publishing Group

Director of Publishing:
Rafael Marfil

Production:
Manel Sánchez

INTRODUCTION, 6

CHAPTER 1: THE HISTORY OF BOOKBINDING, 8

Cont

ents

Introduction

This book provides the reader with a new way to approach the world of bookbinding. Binding, in its simplest form, is the act of sewing together the pages of a written or printed document and protecting it with covers to safeguard it in daily use. There have been some substantial changes in bookbinding throughout history, especially in the areas of decorating and embellishing covers. Sewing and assembly have also been perfected to improve their functionality.

In this book, we don't pretend to include all the history as well as the technical and decorative processes that have developed up to the present. Still, we do intend to present an informative overview for anyone interested in the world of books and bookbinding.

My 20 years of teaching and 35 years of professional involvement in the field have given me broad experience that prepared me to write this book. The text is a result of reflections, questions, problems, and concerns posed to me over the years by bibliophiles and students. It's interesting to note that many of the technical processes and applications in a workshop are done mechanically and are therefore reinforced by experience. The nucleus of this book stems from the need to explain and rationalize processes during the course of teaching and regular contact with bibliophiles.

This book begins with an overview of the history of bookbinding, which is not well known. Next, a chapter on materials and tools introduces you to the different steps that make up bookbinding in the proper sense, from humble books with flexible covers to hardcover bindings. Protective enclosures, which are in vogue these days, make it possible to preserve the books and documents inside while retaining their originality and the stamp of time. The book continues with some restoration information concerning making minor repairs in the workshop. It concludes with a section devoted to decorating the outside of a book, in which some of the many applicable techniques are explained.

This book has been designed not only for people who wish to learn the profession, whether as an amateur or a professional, but also for bibliophiles, collectors, historians, and others. We hope that this book will serve all of you well.

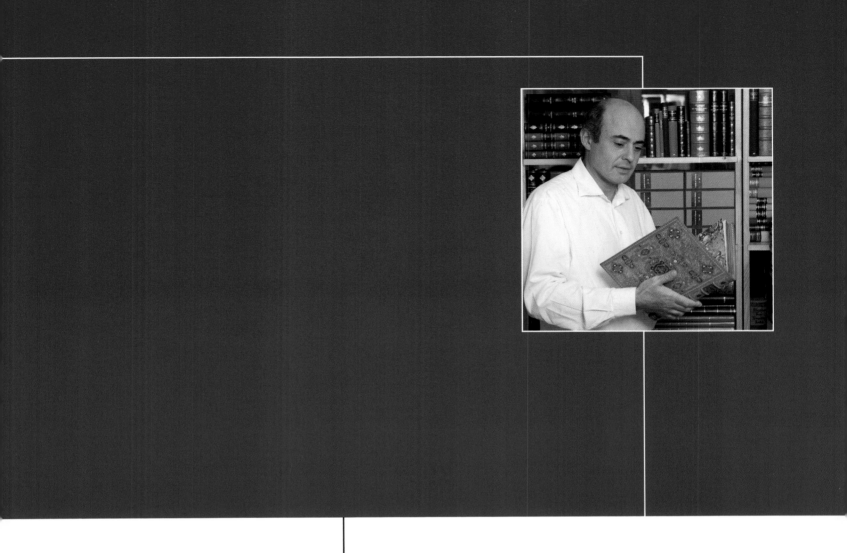

Josep Cambras Riu (born in Barcelona, Spain, 1954) has been a professor of bookbinding at the Arts and Crafts School of the Council of Barcelona since 1985. He has also presented seminars in Havana, Cuba, at the request of the City Museum. He began his professional activities as a devotee of the most significant bookbinders and gilders in Barcelona. Since that time he has upheld the classical techniques of the craft, adapting them to new technologies and materials. During his years as a professional bookbinder, his workshop has produced major bindings of high artistic and bibliographical merit alongside humbler bindings. He treats all books with equal respect, regardless of their economic value.

Riu has taken part in the most prestigious expositions on modern bookbinding held in cities such as Monaco, Quebec, Luxembourg, Athens, Madrid, and others. In 2001, the Autonomous Government of Cataluña presented him with a degree as Master Bookbinder.

His prestige in this field has enabled him to present conferences in specialized bookbinding at bibliophilic centers and participate in round tables dealing with various audiovisual media. His works are featured in some of the most important private libraries in Europe, plus public institutions such as the Library of Cataluña, the National Library in Madrid, the Crown Archive in Aragón, and others.

B ookbinding is a subject that is unfamiliar to most people. Thus, its history and general importance are even less well known. In spite of broad appreciation of the content of books, it's quite common for the styles, historical relevance, and actual value of old bindings to remain obscure. It's regrettable that these ancient works are not appreciated as they could be, and this section sheds light on the subject in an attempt to raise awareness. The history of bookbinding is also useful in furthering our understanding of the development of traditions and techniques still in use today. The practical knowledge gained from historical models makes it possible to recreate these bindings. Studying this subject also adds to the greater appreciation of works that bookbinders from all ages have contributed to us.

The History of *Bookbinding*

Books are assemblies of handwritten or printed pages joined together to form an orderly volume for consultation or reading. Bookbinding arose as a means to assemble and handle these pages. This craft makes it easier to use them, preserve them for longer periods of time, and present them in a more attractive fashion. In many instances, the book's binding attains the level of a true work of art.

Origins

The modern concept of bookbinding began with the appearance of the codex or manuscript book around the first century AD. These books look similar to the ones we know today. Even before this time, highly valued writings were compiled in different forms to protect them with a binding.

Primary materials used for ancient manuscripts include Mesopotamian and Syrian tablets made from tree bark or wood layered with wax on which to write, plant fibers (such as papyrus), monumental inscriptions on stone or metal plates, and processed hides (such as parchment).

In most cases, these brief texts required no protection. Surfaces used for writing varied in difficulty of use and price, leading to distinct specializations. Thus, the most important texts, such as laws and edicts, commonly ended up on monumental forms, such as steles (a stone slab with an inscription or design used as a monument or grave marker). Less important texts were stored in libraries and archives.

Scrolls and clay tablets were the most common writings archived and conserved prior to codices. Scrolls were particularly important since they made up the legendary libraries of Alexandria and Pergamum. The materials used, such as papyrus, were fragile, and in certain instances leather tubes were used to protect and transport them. This system evidently was not exclusive to papyrus, since it is still used today for scrolls containing the sacred Hebrew books.

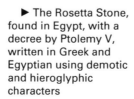

▲ Stele of Adad-nenari III (810-783 BC)

Frequently, since the scrolls lacked external protection, they were commonly folded in the shape of a double roll so that one part was unrolled as it was read, while the other was wound onto the other section. The band that held them together might contain a label with the work's name that made it possible to identify it when on a library shelf.

The Romans also used this system because it facilitated the writing and transport of texts while preserving them in libraries and archives essential to the functioning of the administration.

► The Rosetta Stone, found in Egypt, with a decree by Ptolemy V, written in Greek and Egyptian using demotic and hieroglyphic characters

Scrolls were gradually replaced by codices (manuscript volumes) as early as the first century AD. This essential change grew out of circumstances that modified the form of the book and its binding. There was a need to bind increasingly long works together so that the writings could be more effectively used. Also, papyrus was limiting as a material for preserving books. And, the advent of Christianity affected the overall importance of books.

This new religion used extensive writings considered to be the word of God. To spread the liturgy, it seemed essential for every church to have a copy of the Bible. Likewise, people needed to know how to read and write in order to interpret the scripture correctly. But soon there was more to this development than the accommodation of text, and books were appreciated as sacred and precious objects. Many books resulted from valued texts too long to be inscribed on a monument. As a result, these texts were given the most sumptuous treatment possible, highlighting their importance to the faith. This factor was highly influential in the development of books during the Middle Ages, which led to highly appreciated, expensive books that were considered to be true works of art. This series of events was the beginning of luxury bindings carried out in a systematic way.

Schools of Bookbinding

During the Middle Ages in the West, there were several basic schools of bookbinding:

• **Altar bindings** contained the readings for mass. Because they were highly valued, they were often made from exotic materials, including precious or semiprecious stones, or inlays of glass or enamel. Sculpted marble or cameos were commonly added and applied to a wood substrate.

• **Byzantine bindings** with wood covers were lined with costly fabrics (sometimes tapestries or dyed fabrics) and lots of enamel. This type of binding began to feature decoration based on religious themes, including the figurative imagery, which was rare in Islam.

• **Mudejar style bindings** were made of wood covered with leather. Usually associated with workshops influenced by Islam, this type of binding is very common in the countries of the Iberian Peninsula.

• **Parchment bindings** of lesser value were usually made from wood covers with very simple decoration or none at all, and no covering—reinforced with metallic protections or decorations. Parchment was commonly used for frequently used documents and books that were not essential to preserve.

▲ Plateresque style with metal corner pieces and decorations

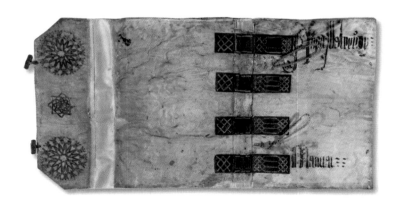

► Parchment binding in the form of a folder (16th century)

▲ Mudejar style with metal closures and decorations

▲ Altar binding with gold and enamel

Bindings on Islamic Manuscripts

The Islamic world, like the Christian world, had needs related to written material. Very early on, a corpus was assembled containing interpretations of the doctrine transmitted by the prophet Muhammad. This compilation came to be known as the Koran. It was a true book that needed to be remembered, known, and spread throughout all of Islam. Based on this religious need, it became necessary to know how to read, write, study, and interpret the writings to gain access to the religious teachings. The Koran was also used as a basic text to teach Arabs how to read and write. It was also used to teach Arabic to the faithful who spoke different native languages.

Thus, two essential factors affected the dissemination of bookbinding in the Islamic world: an extensive number of books were produced and therefore in need of protection due to their value. Also, the tremendously important Koran required more elaborate treatment and was regarded as an elevated object.

From the standpoint of form, the first Arab bindings owe a lot to the Coptic bindings that preceded them. Books bound in leather containing applied decorative elements were known in Christian Egypt; some included tooling and others were decorated with gold using the technique of *guilloche*. The earliest-known examples are from the sixth century, which are now housed in the Coptic Museum (Cairo, Egypt). The first Islamic bindings are clearly related to these examples. The Muslims developed and perfected what was learned from this tradition. These bindings are far more widespread, and Arab literature

▲ Example of Persian folder binding (14th century)

describes the medieval techniques and tools that were used. We know that the Arabs used fleurons/rosettes, tooling, and fillets. They also used decorative techniques such as onlays, gilding, and painted leather.

Due to the custom of avoiding figures representing animals or humans in connection with religion, plant and geometric motifs dominate this decoration. This decoration is often complex and contains many interlaced motifs. Islamic bindings incorporate the typical envelope or folder form—in other words, there is a flap that closes the binding through a slit to provide greater protection.

This type of binding was centered in Egypt and Syria. It was also found in Muslim Spain, from which it was carried to the Christian lands. Later it was centered in 15th- and 16th-century Persia and the Ottoman and Muslim states of India in a form similar to that of the West. However, without the benefit of printing, the diffusion of books and their social role was significantly different. Beginning in the 14th century, gilding was practiced in Persia. This very significant development seems to have moved from there to the peninsular countries and spread throughout Italy and France well into the 15th century.

◄ Islamic binding (15th century)

When the Gutenberg press was developed in the 15th century, another essential change in books and their bindings came about—the gradual appearance and eventual dominance of the printed book. This development helped to bring about a series of changes to the form of books. To begin with, books became much more accessible and homogenous. They distanced themselves from the excessively expensive, handmade, and elitist products that had characterized prior medieval books. They were no longer considered to be works exclusively of great value requiring a major investment for their preservation. They were less expensive works identical to many others without the need for great protection. This reduced the importance of binding at this time, even though it would recover later on with a different value and purpose. The binding came to serve the purpose of distinguishing one book and its owner from the other copies. The mere possession of a book was no longer a sufficient distinguishing factor for an owner, and it became necessary to personalize and highlight his books. This was done by extolling his name, emblem, or motto, and taste through the incorporation of motifs that symbolized the owner, usually in the form of an emblem or medallion in the book's center.

Many of the Plateresque-style bindings of the Renaissance are decorated with wheels, forming two or three rectangles inscribed inside one another with a central emblem. In Spain, bookbinding exhibited a strong personality highly influenced by Mudejar decorations and less figurative than bookbinding in other locations. During the same period, some editors such as Aldus of Venice, referred to as Aldines, marketed books with luxurious bindings that set off the work, just as they took pains with other details such as typography, editing, and engravings.

◀ Venetian binding (1562)

▲ Renaissance binding (16th century)

◀ Aldine decoration (16th century)

▶ Plateresque style with gold tooling

Renaissance Bindings

The developments we've described so far gave rise to high-quality Renaissance bindings. In these bindings, lighter materials such as pasteboard replaced the wood to which the leather was attached. Precious materials on books gradually fell out of favor. Thus, from the former gold, enamel, and expensive fabrics remained leather, gilding, and so forth—all used on lighter and smaller books. Raised bands were diminished, and smaller metal fittings were used to make the books more elegant. These bindings were distributed broadly, especially in France. For example, Jean Grolier put together a famous library with some 3,000 beautifully bound books. Three well-defined styles appeared: the classical style of Italy, the heavily Islamic style of Spain, and the intricately tooled style of France. The French developments predicted modern styles.

From the standpoint of bookbinding, 17th century turned into a strange period, since it was an era dominated by great religious wars in all of Europe that were closely tied to political struggles for dominance. Books played an essential role in this context. On the one hand, the Protestants spread the Bible through austere, cheap, and abundant books. Consequently, they weren't interested in luxury in either the book or the binding. Also, due to the Austrian monarchy and the Inquisition, there was a profound distrust of books, with the exception of literature for entertainment. This political influence tried to distance editorial production from the Iberian Peninsula, concentrating it in easier to control and less dangerous Flanders and Venice.

This political environment affected editorial production and bookbinding from the end of the 16th through the 17th century. French bookbinding became a model for others to imitate, or at least the moving force for new styles copied throughout much of Europe. Consequently, the decoration on books became lighter and more elegant. Red morocco leather was commonly used. During this period in France, regulations were developed for the bookbinding profession.

Several well-defined styles stand out from this period: The first is known as *à la fanfarre*, made up of three parallel fillets that set off the decorated area with small gilded fleurons/rosettes. The second is the *semé* style, made up of a repetition of a single small gilt fleuron/rosette (generally a fleur-de-lis). The third, developed in mid-17th century, was a binding known as *à la Duseuil*, featuring a field marked off by three fillets with a fleuron/rosette in each of the angles and a motif from heraldry or arms in the center.

Another characteristic 17th-century style is known as fan decoration. This motif was similar to the one from the previous century, but it shows a central rectangle decorated with four fan-shaped motifs. This decorative motif predominated in Spanish binding beginning in the 16th century, before becoming more widespread in French and Italian binding during the next century. Leather onlay decoration also became widespread during this period.

▲ *Officium Beatae Mariae Virginis* (1652), illustrating fan decoration

▲ Renaissance binding (16th century)

The French Model

France, which was on the verge of establishing its continental hegemony, was the one country that escaped this rarified climate of fanaticism and violence. The French demonstrated their taste for culture and books by developing important libraries brimming with carefully edited and bound books. These libraries, owned by the nobility, were connected to the administration and centralized state beginning to take shape in Versailles.

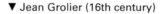

▼ Jean Grolier (16th century)

▲ Beautiful *à la fanfarre* binding (early 17th century)

The 18th Century: The Perfection of Books

The 18th century is often defined as the century of illustration, and in short, as the century of books. This definition applies not only to the number of books produced but the quality of their contents. During this century, there was great freedom in editing and thought, and the printing quality was unprecedented. The bindings of this time are also outstanding, particularly those created in Spain. In France, the new Bourbon kings corrected the dreadful Austrian policy toward books, favoring, in the image of France, editorial production, diffusion, and protection of books. Philip V, king of Spain (1700-1746), issued a decree prohibiting the importation of bound books. The covers of foreign books entering the country were ripped off, in spite of the furious protests of booksellers. This climate was the point of departure for the development of an original style of bookbinding. The royal court and State both became good clients, protectors, and patrons of bookbinding. The work of Antonio de Sancha stands out during this period. He was a court bookseller, editor, and binder and an exceptional gilder.

During this time, France was the point of reference for bookbinding, but other styles gradually gained prominence. The English style imitated the form of the French bindings, but treated them with a personalized style. The raised bands were inconspicuous, the title was generally placed on the spine, and a fillet or decorated roll was commonly used on the covers' edges. Morocco leathers were commonly used, particularly red, but olive green, blue, and even yellow were used as well. In addition, leather onlays were incorporated more frequently.

Bookbinding during this period, referred to in France as *à la dentelle*, was developed by Padeloup, the binder to the court of Louis XV, who served as a model for all of Europe. He used a binding composed of a multitude of tiny interlaced pieces of metal to make an ornamental border, or applied a decorated roll to imitate this effect. Ornamental fleurons/rosettes and curved shapes domnated in accord with the reigning rococo style—shapes that were simplified during the reign of Louis XVI. The central motif was usually compatible and similar.

◄ A marvelous example of the Imperial style (18th century)

► *Dentelle* (18th century)

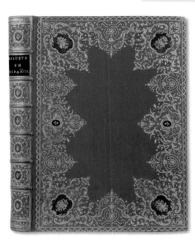

▼ A beautiful curtain-style binding (18th century)

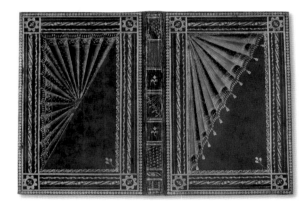

During this period, low-quality parchment binding declined. "Cheap" bindings made of pasteboard, and especially so-called Spanish board binding, were used with increasing frequency. The end of the *Ancien Régime*, due to the Revolution, caused a period of decline in luxury bindings, produced in other countries, including Spain. One of the top bookbinders was Gabriel de Sancha, son of Antonio, who had studied the craft in Paris and London. Other highly talented bookbinders of this period included Gabriel Gómez.

The 19th Century and the First Industrial Productions

This century was a climactic century for books and literature. Books had never been as widely dispersed. During this century, they were transformed into a medium of culture, amusement, information, and more. This phenomenon was due in part to the growth of industrialization, which made books cheaper to print in unprecedented numbers, placing them within reach of a significant portion of the population. In essence, they became objects of consumerism.

This development made bookbinding more esoteric. Luxury bindings were still created for the purpose of distinguishing and highlighting certain books and libraries, and only editorial bindings of high quality were created, reflecting the art and aesthetics of the time.

As a result of these changes, inferior bindings made merely to protect the book contrasted with extraordinarily high-quality bindings by great bookbinders.

▲ Antonio de Sancha (18th century)

◀ Industrial binding, full leather (Menard, 19th century)

This industrialization process was very complex, leading to profound changes in the world of books. This shift was completely in place toward the end of the century, but it was a slow process with various phases of formation and development.

Imperial and Romantic Binding

Two styles of bookbinding developed reflecting tendencies halfway between those of 18th-century binding and those of the latter 19th century. The former, known as Imperial binding, was very similar to the bindings of the previous period with different "à la mode" motifs. Sober decorations and simple fleurons/rosettes juxtaposed with classical and Egyptian motifs. In Spain, bindings had a curtain-like motif and were referred to by that term. These bindings, developed mainly by Valencian bookbinders, rose in significance.

Romantic or cathedral bookbinding was partially mass-produced and characteristically displayed images from Gothic cathedrals. Sometimes the binding image was created with finishing tools, but many times the images were done with metal die-stamps in a partially mass-produced binding.

Bindings with mottled pasteboard covers also became fashionable and were often done in gold-embossed half leather. In Spain, "*Rocaille*" and curvilinear motifs were popular on bindings, particularly during the reign of Isabel II.

During this period, another characteristically Spanish binding became widespread. Valencian board binding was apparently invented by José Beneyto in the 18th century and perfected by Antonio Suárez. This system used leather treated with acid to imitate the effects of the mottled papers that were already very common at the time.

In addition, between 1870 and the end of the century, some excellent mass-produced industrial bindings were made with metal die-stamping. In Barcelona, E. Domènech, and prestigious publishers such as Espasa and Company and Montaner and Simón produced outstanding examples of this type of binding.

The Arts and Crafts Movement

During the closing years of the 19th century, there was a reaction against the dominance of mass-produced books and bindings. Connected to the Arts and Crafts movement, this philosophy sought to revive craft traditions and traditional methods in all artistic mediums, including bookbinding. Thus, two types of deluxe binding came into fashion: those referred to as "historic" that attempted to combine the books' content with the binding's frequently historical motifs; and others done by hand, but closely linked to the predominant aesthetic movements of the period. In the former type of binding, medieval styles and copies of earlier bookbinding styles were prominent within an aesthetic movement dominated by historicism. The latter type maintained a fondness for the craft traditions, tending to adapt the current aesthetic to bookbinding.

◀ Valencian board binding

▶ Spectacular binding in the cathedral style with gold tooling, leather onlays, and gauffering (19th century)

The 20th Century: The Book as a Consumer Object

During the 20th century, the mass production of books that began in the 19th century reached its ultimate peak. Books almost entirely lost their value as cultural references. Instead, they were replaced by the mass phenomena of "disposables," such as bestsellers and other popular books.

Today, there are still some carefully made editions of books that bibliophiles collect. But, generally speaking, it's clear that the social role of books, and therefore of binding, has changed dramatically. From our point of view, we feel that this change has raised questions once more about all aspects of bookbinding—from traditional handwork to industrial binding, with the latter increasingly focused on colors and aggressive designs that are able to attract the attention of consumers. On the other hand, the evolution of what is considered to be "art" during the 20th century has also affected books. For example, there has been an extraordinary development of artists' books that are no longer connected to traditional bibliophily or a particular style of book decoration, but rather to artistic book-making. In this context, books are considered to be objects and a visual medium like any other, with value unrelated to content. There are, of course, many examples that fall in between these two extremes.

A Renewed Sensitivity

At the beginning of the 20th century, production bindings of high quality, paralleled by modern art, placed new emphasis on bookbinding by relating it to contemporary artistic movements and distancing it from preceding historicisms. J. Figueroa of Barcelona played an essential role in this development. In essence, industrial and handmade binding became clearly separated, allowing the latter more room to develop its own brilliance. In the first half of

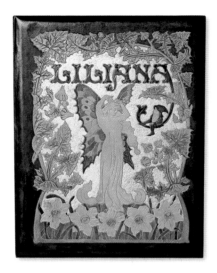

▲ Modernist style by Figuerola, 1907

the century, there was a rich tradition of bookbinding influenced by art movements such as Art Deco, Modernism, *Noucentism*, and various avant-garde movements.

In the second half of the century, a general interest in bookbinding reappeared, fostered by a middle class that was sensitive to the world of culture and interested in grand libraries. It was a brilliant period for bookbinding because a style developed on its own that was removed from the previous experimental and artistic "à la mode" currents. Eclectic hand-crafted bookbinding was guided by the book's theme and a large dose of historicism. Important figures include Brugalla in Barcelona, Galván in Cádiz, and Palomino in Madrid. All of them had a refined craft technique that stood apart from contemporary artistic movements.

Contemporary Bookbinding

The overriding use of computers and the Internet in today's world has fostered a debate about the role of books and bookbinding. It's clear that these developments force a fresh look at the subject. It's possible that books will be published in a different format in the future. Nevertheless, there is a tremendous number of valuable books already published that won't go away and will need binding. As a result, it seems possible that books will gain importance as objects.

The idea of books as objects of distinction and culture developed during the middle of the 20th century when bookbinding flourished but was progressively abandoned toward the end of the century. In addition, it became even more difficult to define the role of the artistic book-object, due to a certain lack of definition within artistic movements. Today, the climate seems to point to redefining bookbinding's role. Perhaps the following types of craft bookbinding will exist in the future: a pragmatic one, a classical one, and finally, one created through artistic experimentation.

▲ Paul Bonet, *The Death of Venice*, 1937

◄ Figurative binding by Josep Cambras

*T*he tools used in bookbinding can be divided roughly by size. In the following chapter, large tools are grouped with the equipment used for bookbinding. There are sometimes alternatives for the larger tools and equipment, but they don't always create superior work. The small tools described in this chapter assist you in carrying out a variety of bookbinding procedures.

Many of the tools used in craft binding have remained the same over time, even though some have been improved with respect to function and precision. In addition, a wide variety of materials with many finishes are available for covering books. The many bookbinding adhesives on the market, made to fill different needs, are discussed separately in this chapter.

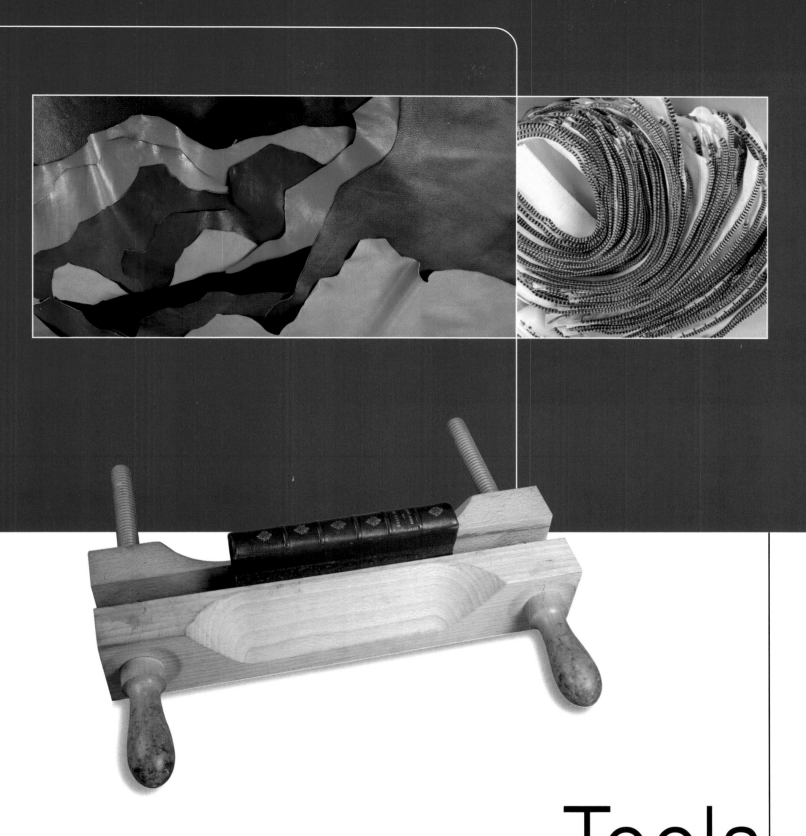

Tools
and Materials

Equipment, Materials, and Tools

▲ Board shear with a tray for binders' board off-cuts

Equipment

Board Shear

This tool works like a pair of large scissors with one arm attached to the edge of the worktable. The other arm has a handle, a pivot, and an attached counterweight. It is used mainly to make right-angle cuts in binders' board and paper. Board shears come in many sizes, from small paper cutters used in offices to larger ones with a cutting blade over 3 feet (.9 m) long.

Small paper cutters are inadequate for cutting thick binders' board. For that purpose, you'll need a board shear with a blade at least 31 inches long (78.7 cm), which is the minimum width of the board. The board shear should have a sturdy foot clamp to hold the board in position while you cut it. Keep the blades sharp and in good condition for optimum performance.

The cutter should also have a metal strip marked off in units of measurement running parallel to the cut to guide you when you trim the board to the desired size.

The Guillotine

This machine is used to make precision cuts. Since it is a large and expensive machine, people have tried to find alternatives; but the quality, speed, and neatness of the cut it produces are without equal. There are both manual and electric guillotines that are similarly constructed—both have a sharp steel blade that drops down at an angle to the horizontal plane and a cast frame supported by a strong table with four legs.

Both types have a clamp that descends vertically to hold the book or the pages securely on the flat surface of the guillotine table. They have a backstop parallel to the cut line that can be moved forward or backward with a crank to adjust it to the size of the cut. In addition, a stop perpendicular to the cut line is secured to the machine. To execute a perfectly square cut, the book has to be held tightly against the two stops.

The Lying Press and Plough

This tool is used in place of the guillotine for trimming books. It's a lying press with a blade called a plough that slides between guides attached to the press. These guides are commonly located on the side opposite of that used for "backing" (forming the spine and shoulders of) books. The handle on the plough must rotate to perform the trimming action. It's advisable to use a square to be sure the book is trimmed straight.

◄ An electric guillotine

▼ Hot stamping press used for embossing covers

▲ Standing press

The Standing Press

This press, equipped with an iron wheel, is a fundamental, frequently used piece of equipment in the bookbinder's workshop. It's usually secured to a wooden or solid steel bench with a cabinet to store the boards. Because of the way the press is designed, it's possible to apply varying degrees of pressure for different binding procedures that range from strong pressure for laminating binders' board, to gentle pressure to prevent the book from warping during the drying process.

These presses have two basic features: a fixed structure at the base and a movable element in the upper part that exerts the pressure.

▼ Lying press with iron "backing" boards

The Hot Stamping Press

This press is used for embossing book covers in gold using heated metal dies. The press has an electrical device for heating it that keeps the die at the appropriate temperature for successful stamping.

The Lying Press

This basic tool of the bookbinder's workshop is used in various procedures, including trimming book edges with the plough and backing books. This heavy, horizontal press has a span of about 24 inches (61 cm) between the screws to accommodate fairly large books. It is held firmly in position in a wooden base called a "tub."

The Tools

The smallest tools used in bookbinding can be bought or even made at home, but some of them, such as a bone folder and paring knife, can be highly personalized. There are many tools used in various bookbinding procedures. Some are used for just one step, and others are used throughout the binding of the book. Tools used most frequently are kept close at hand on the workbench.

▲ Beveled boards for applying pressure when gilding book edges

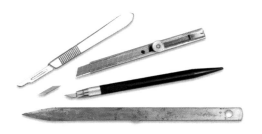

▲ Small cutting tools that are also used in book restoration

▲ Bookbinding hammer, used for rounding and backing book spines

▼ Various saws for making saw-kerfs across the back-folds of the signatures in preparation for sewing

Disbinding a Previously Sewn Book for Rebinding

The following tools will be helpful in taking the book apart:

• **Binder's knife**. This common tool is used to remove the leftover glue and cut the sewing threads of the old binding.

• **Scalpel**. You'll use a scalpel in several parts of the binding process. We recommend keeping two sizes of replacement blades on hand: a fairly fine one and a heavier one for cuts that require more force.

• **Artist's brush**. A $^1/2$-inch (1.3 cm) brush is useful for pasting up spines or repairing damaged signatures.

Creating Saw-kerfs

The essential tools for this particular step in binding are the following:

• **Back saw**. Use this saw to make saw-kerfs across the back-folds of the signatures in preparation for sewing.

• **Wooden boards**. Beech or oak boards are used to hold the signatures in the lying press during sawing. As an alternative, you can use pieces of binders' board.

• **Pencils**. Keep a couple on hand for marking the sawing guides on the spine.

• **Template**. This is a simple card with markings indicating the placement of the saw-kerfs on the book's spine.

Sewing

For proper sewing, you need to have the following tools:

• **Sewing frame**. This piece of equipment is composed of a small stationary wooden table on four feet. On either end are two wooden screws and nuts attached perpendicular to the table. On the upper part of the screws is a crossbar to which the sewing supports are attached.

• **Needles**. These must be long and strong, without sharp points. The eyes need to be large enough to accommodate the thread easily, but not so large that they damage the signature as they are pulled through the hole.

• **Sewing keys**. These small items are used to secure the cords or cloth tapes under the table of the sewing frame. As a substitute, you can use some small pieces of binders' board with small cuts to keep the cord from slipping, or use a few long nails.

▲ Sewing keys keep the supports under tension in the setup of the sewing frame.

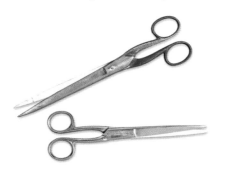

▲ Various types of scissors are essential in the workshop

• **Sewing hooks**. These are made of metal and used to secure the cord or cloth sewing tape to the sewing frame. Thumbtacks can be substituted for the keys if necessary.

• **Graduated ruler**. For measuring, choose a stainless-steel ruler between 1 and 2 feet long (30.5-61 cm), graduated in sixty-fourths of an inch (millimeters).

• **Scissors**. You won't need large scissors for use with the sewing that you do in bookbinding, but they need to be 8 inches (20.3 cm) long or more. Desk scissors are very useful for this task.

For Decorating Edges

Decorating edges, especially gilding, is a somewhat forgotten technique. Some books are colored on top, followed by burnishing, since this helps to protect the book from dust. Here are the tools needed for decorating the edges:

• **Steel scraper**. This tool is a blade of thin steel rounded on one side and flat on the other that is available in several sizes. Choose one that best suits the size of the book. The rounded side of the scraper is for the concave fore edge, and the flat one is for the top and bottom edges. You can also use fine sandpaper to do this job.

• **Agate burnisher**. This tool has a wooden handle with a head that is usually made of a flat or rounded agate that corresponds to the shape of the edge being burnished. It is used for burnishing waxed, colored, or gilded edges.

• **Frame with wire mesh**. This tool, used with a brush, is used for speckling the edges of the book with a contrasting color—a style that was once common on accounting books.

For Fraying Out Cords

It's a good idea to have all of the tools listed below for fraying out the sewing cord extensions before forwarding the book.

• **Fraying board**. This is a thin piece of wood with a notch 1 inch (2.5 cm) long in it through which the cord is passed before it is frayed to protect the bookblock. A thin metal piece in the same shape will also work for this purpose.

• **Dull knife**. This knife with a dull blade is used for undoing and fraying the sewing cord extensions so they don't form lumps on the cover boards.

• **Awl**. This tool consists of a strong needle with a wooden handle, and it is used for making holes in the board for the cords to lace through. It can also be used for making small holes for "dog-tooth" oversewing.

◄ A rasp for fraying cords, a card, and a knife

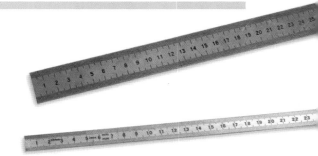

▲ Flat metal rulers are more often used for cutting and marking than measuring.

▲ Different types of agate burnishers are used for gilding book edges.

▲ An awl is used in making holes in binders' board and paper.

For Assembling the Book

This process can vary in some steps, depending on the technique used (hollow back, tight back, etc.). Making leather covers that require special tools will be treated separately. For assembling the book, you'll need the following:

• **Pressing boards**. These are made of wood or laminates and are about 1/2-inch thick (1.3 cm). They should be larger than the book that is to be pressed. It's also a good idea to have some large, waterproof boards on hand to use for restoration.

• **Artist's brushes or other small brushes**. Keep a few of these on hand in different sizes for gluing spines, board, etc., with adhesive or starch paste. Buy good quality brushes, otherwise they'll deteriorate rapidly. Each brush must be used for a specific type of adhesive: for instance, one round brush with stiff bristles for resin adhesives, another for heated animal glue, and another for starch paste.

• **Bookbinder's hammer**. This tool is used for "backing" the book spine to consolidate and create shoulders.

• **Bone folder**. This is a bone or wooden tool, often with one rounded and one pointed end. It should be a little over 6 inches long (15.2 cm) and about 1 inch wide (2.5 cm). Other sizes and shapes are also quite useful. Its original use was for folding signatures, but it is useful for many other bookbinding procedures as well.

• **Files or rasps**. These are used for beveling the board.

• **Sandpaper**. Several grades of sandpaper are used for smoothing book spines and board edges. In some cases, it's preferable to glue the sandpaper to a wood block for more precise work.

▼ Folders made of wood and bone are indispensable for the workshop because they're used during the entire process of making a book.

▼ A wood file for beveling the boards

• **Spine former**. Used to shape the spines of books, this wooden tool with concave grooves of various sizes is accompanied by a wooden instrument with rounded ends.

• **Hot glue pot**. Originally, this pot was a double boiler used to liquefy animal glue without burning it. Today, glue pots are usually electric, and the temperature is controlled by means of a thermostat.

• **Paste containers**. These containers hold the starch paste, with a bar or cord in the middle for squeezing out the bristles. They have to be washable, since the paste deteriorates quickly.

• **Metal weights**. These are used for light pressing.

• **Pressing rods**. These long, narrow rods of stainless steel, wood, or plastic are made in various thicknesses and used in pairs to form the grooves of a cloth-covered book. Knitting needles are also useful for this purpose.

For Leather Bindings

For working with leather bindings, you'll need a few special tools that are not used with cloth covers. For trimming down the leather, you'll need the following:

• **Paring stone**. A smooth stone used for paring and thinning down leather. It must be very smooth to avoid damaging or marking the surface of the tanned leather. A lithographic stone can be used, or if none is available, use thick tempered plate glass with a skid-proof backing to prevent it from slipping during use.

• **Paring knife**. A cutting tool with a handle and a steel blade that is about $1^1/2$ inches wide (3.8 cm) and 7 inches long (17.8 cm). The beveled blade is either rounded or angled and must be kept sharp.

• **Band nippers**. A tool used to form the leather over raised bands on leather bindings.

▶ Lithographic stone and paring knives used to thin leather. The stone is framed in a wooden support that keeps it from sliding on the table.

▲ Gluing sandpaper to a block of wood or binders' board makes it easier to handle. Sandpaper is sold in different grades.

▲ The spine-former is used to create the curve in the book's spine.

▲ Band nippers are used for fitting the leather over the raised bands on the spine.

▲ Brass leather burnisher mounted in a long wooden handle that can be held against your shoulder as you use it

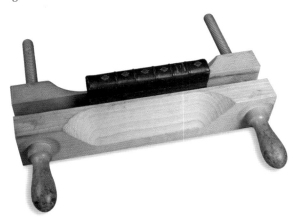

◄ Gas finishing stoves can be used to heat the tools to the right temperature.

• **Burnisher**. This tool is usually made of brass and has an arched and rounded point. A long wooden handle allows you to rest it on your shoulder. After heating it, use it to burnish the spines of leather-bound books.

Gold Tooling

This technique, which involves tooling with gold leaf, requires some special instruments and materials. The following list includes tools for handling the delicate gold leaf and tooling:

• **Finishing press**. This is a small horizontal press made of beech with two wooden screws that apply pressure and hold the book in place during gold tooling.

• **Gold cushion**. Used for laying out and cutting the gold leaf sheets, this cushion is made from a rectangular piece of board about 5 x 10 inches (12.7 x 25.4 cm) covered by tightly stretched leather (rough-side up). It is cushioned with horsehair or fine cotton.

• **Gold knife**. This knife for cutting and manipulating gold leaf should have a long, straight blade about 10 inches long (25.4 cm).

• **Cover for the gold cushion**. A protective screen made to prevent air currents from disturbing or damaging the gold leaf.

• **Cloth swab**. A cotton ball covered with a piece of cloth gathered and tied at the top serves as a swab. After it is moistened slightly with sweet almond oil, it is used to make the gold adhere to the leather. It also facilitates burnishing the covers.

• **Artist's brushes**. Use very fine, soft brushes to apply glaire to the areas to be tooled in gold.

• **Dividers**. Used for taking and marking measurements, this instrument has two pointed, movable legs with an adjustment screw. You'll need one that is about 6 inches (15.2 cm) long.

• **Finishing stove**. Used for heating the finishing tools to the right temperature, this piece of equipment is usually fueled by gas, but there are also electric versions. A camping stove is an acceptable substitute.

• **Basin**. This shallow container with a sponge in the bottom for retaining moisture is used to cool down the finishing tools if they get too hot.

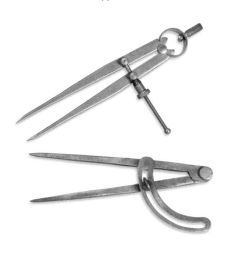

▲ A finishing press is used to hold the book vertically on a table while tooling the spine.

▼ Two different types of metal dividers

▶ Different items used in gilding with gold leaf: sweet almond oil, glaire, a cloth swab, gold knife, gold cushion, and gold leaf

◄ A collection of hand tools

Finishing Tools

Finishing tools come in many shapes and designs. The brass end of the tool has an engraved design that is attached to a wooden handle, making it possible to use the tool when heated. These finishing tools, except for the hand tools, have shapes adapted making them easier to apply to a rounded spine or flat covers. Basic types of finishing tools are described below:

• **Pallet**. This line tool has a slightly curved shape to work more easily on the spine's curvature. It is used to tool lines of different thicknesses and other decorations on a book's spine.

• **Decorative hand tool**. This tool, used for decorating covers, has a design engraved into the brass end. They have a broad selection of ornamental features (floral and heraldic motifs, animals, etc.) and decorative styles (Mudejar, Gothic, baroque, etc.) They can be used individually or in pairs, and are sometimes differentiated for right and left. These tools can be used on both spines and covers of leather-bound books.

• **Lines and gouges**. These tools are used for tooling straight and curved lines on the leather. They customarily come in sets with different sizes. A large set of lines and gouges are needed to accommodate all cover design possibilities.

▼ A set of lines and gouges

• **Fillets and rolls**. These tools are made up of a brass wheel attached to a wooden handle that rests against the shoulder. The fillet has a line or lines engraved on the edge, and the roll has a design engraved on the edge. The wheel is heated and rolled on the leather to emboss the engraved edge in a linear fashion.

• **Metal embossing dies**. These brass, magnesium, or zinc dies, made by photo-engraving, reproduce decorative elements. They are mounted on a hot stamp press, heated, and embossed on covers.

In order to add the title and other textual features, you'll need the following tools:

• **Lettering pallet**. This tool has a wooden handle and a brass, self-centering kind of holder. It is used for tooling the title, author, etc. information on the spine of leather bindings.

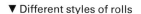

▼ Different styles of rolls

• **Brass type**. A collection of letters used for stamping text on book covers. Each piece of type must be set individually in the lettering pallet or hot stamping press prior to stamping. Brass spacers of different thicknesses accompany each font. It's a good idea to have several different sizes of a particular font. Single brass letters mounted on wooden handles can also be used for titling book covers. These letters are stamped individually.

• **Type case**. This case, divided into compartments, makes it possible to organize the type and spacers of a particular font size.

▶ Various pallets for gold tooling

▶▶ Wooden drawers containing type cases of different sizes and a lettering pallet

The Materials

Endbands

This decorative feature is usually made of fabric in various colors, although sometimes leather is used. It is placed on the spine of the book at the head and tail, and serves to decorate and reinforce the bindings. Simple endbands in two or three colors are the most common, and they can be made by hand or machine-made commercially. For special books, distinctive endbands can be made or embroidered that complement the decorative style dictated by the binding.

Binders' Board

Binders' board was introduced in the 16th century as the structural basis of the binding. Before this time, covers were made from wood. Beginning in the 17th century, binders' board was made of sheets of paper pasted together called "pasteboard." Later, densely pressed binders' board replaced this light board. Gray millboard is a type of binders' board used for bookbinding that is very strong and durable. It is made by machine using scrap paper, hemp cord, and rags. Binders' board is classified according to its thickness and density.

▲Binders' board of different densities and thicknesses are needed in the workshop.

◀ Handmade silk endbands

◄ Check the consistency of glue by noting how much runs off the brush.

▲ A double-boiler hot glue pot. This one has two reservoirs for alternating between thin or thick glue, depending on the requirements of the job.

Adhesives

Adhering is one of the most important aspects of bookbinding, and different adhesives fit various purposes. It's important to make the right choice, because each adhesive has different working properties. Let's take a look at the types of adhesives that can be used:

• **White glue or synthetic adhesive**. Commonly referred to simply as PVA, these adhesives are commonly manufactured using polyvinyl acetate. Today, these adhesives are widely used in many bookbinding processes. They are convenient and have a long shelf life. However, they aren't reversible: once they dry they can only be removed with strong solvents. For that reason, they shouldn't be used on books and paper of artifactual value during restoration or conservation.

• **Hot glue, organic gelatin glue, or carpenter's glue**. This glue is made from animal bones and trimmings. It is sold in flakes or tablets so it will dissolve more easily in water when heated. Use a double boiler for this purpose. When the glue is ready, it will be the color of honey. After this, it will darken and deteriorate if heated for a long time.

• **Starch paste**. This adhesive of plant origin is reversible in water. It remains both clear and flexible after drying. Due to the high percentage of water, it has a high penetrating power and dries slowly, making it suitable for leather bookbinding. It adheres the leather firmly while allowing enough time to complete all of the steps before drying. After a few days, it deteriorates and must be discarded.

Colors for Painting Edges

Generally, water-based aniline dyes are used for coloring the edges, since they don't penetrate the paper easily. To create a color, dissolve the aniline powders in water to make a fairly liquid paste, and keep the solution in a bottle.

► Water-based aniline dyes are used for painting or marbling book edges. Sometimes, although rarely, they are used for dying leathers, such as in a "curtain binding."

▲ Thread and linen cord for sewing books, usually made of linen or cotton

Cords, Tapes, Thread, and Ribbons

A book can be sewn using either cords or tapes, depending on the type of binding and how easily the book must open.

• **Cords**. The best cords are made of linen or hemp, rather than jute, since they are of better quality. Cords come in various thicknesses and are selected with respect to the size and weight of the book.

• **Tapes**. To provide greater elasticity and ease of opening for certain bindings, tapes are used as sewing supports rather than cords. These are made of either cotton or linen; the most common ones are from about $1/2$ to $3/4$-inch wide (1.3 to 1.9 cm).

• **Thread**. It's customary to use linen thread for sewing the book.

• **Ribbons**. These can be incorporated into special books where they'll be useful for keeping the reader's place. These are fine bands of silk or satin, either colored or decorated, that are glued onto the spine at the head.

Paper

Various kinds of paper are used within a single book, from the paper used in the body of the book to those used for assembly and decoration. Each paper has its own characteristics that bookbinders should keep in mind when choosing one.

All the paper materials must have their grain running parallel to the spine for a book to close properly and prevent the covers from warping and flyleaves from wrinkling. With machine-made papers, the paper fibers run in one direction. Handmade paper, on the other hand, has fibers that fall in many directions. When the paper absorbs moisture during pasting, it expands parallel to the direction of the fibers.

• **The direction of the grain**. Bend paper gently to check the direction of its grain. If it bends easily, you've found the direction of the fiber; otherwise the paper will be resistant and tend to crinkle.

In bookbinding, various types of paper are classified according to their use in different processes. For end sheets, it is important to use strong, high-quality paper. Either a handmade or machine-made laid paper can be used. Heavy artist's papers and other fine papers are good choices, and they are available in subdued colors. These papers can be used for both end sheets as well as covers and slipcases. In today's marketplace, there's a broad selection of papers for every need. Choose the thickness and quality of the paper to fit the binding.

• **Newsprint**. Clean newsprint is economical and very useful in protecting your bench while pasting up cloth, leather, and paper.

▼ Colored papers are useful for endsheets, boxmaking, and slipcases.

Strong, durable paper is used for strengthening spines and making hollow tubes. Unfortunately, Kraft or wrapping paper is very commonly used for this task, although it is very acidic and can damage the document.

You can use decorated papers to embellish a book (both the covers and the flyleaves) and for making slipcases. These papers are sold in countless varieties. Bookbinders also decorate their own paper. Papers can be stamped by hand, marbled, or decorated with tinted paste. They can also be printed xylographically with a wood engraving or woodcut block. Any paper used for a protective function must be strong with colors stable enough to prevent the decoration from smudging when adhesive is applied to the back.

• **Special papers**. In some cases, you'll need other types of special papers, including those that can help in repairing small imperfections. For small restorations, you'll use Japanese tissue.

▼ Sampler of fabrics and papers of different colors and textures

▲ Marbled papers, handmade by Montse Buxó

Fabrics

Fabrics used in bookbinding can be divided into two groups: those needed for constructing the book, and those used for covering the book (bookcloth and buckram).

• **Mull**. Used mainly for reinforcing the spine of books, this cotton material has a broad weave and substance.

• **Linen reinforcement cloth**. This linen cloth is thin and strong. In comparison to mull, it is more tightly woven and has a smoother texture. It is used for reinforcement in books and slipcovers as well and making joints and hinges.

• **Bookcloth**. This material is used for covering books and slipcovers. It consists of cotton fabric in various colors specially treated or lined with paper to keep the adhesive from bleeding through. The fabric, like paper and binders' board, has a grain direction that might need to be considered in cutting and adhering the material.

In addition to the fabric backed by paper, a great many materials with different textures, finishes, and colors are now available that imitate cloth and leather. Usually durable and easy to use, they take adhesive well and are suited for embossing. These materials are known by their commercial names. All these materials are used for simple economical bindings.

▼ Bookbinding fabrics with paper backings are easy to adhere.

Leathers

Leathers are the material par excellence for covering books, whether only the spine or the entire cover. Traditionally, different types of leather have been used, depending on the type of binding or time period. Today, commonly used leathers are goatskin, and in some cases, dressed sheepskin or parchment.

Hides used for bookbinding are usually tanned with organic material to give them the proper strength and workability. Leathers are sold in various categories of quality based on any defects they might have (scars, marks, etc.), and they are usually sold by the square foot, a measurement that is marked on the flesh side. A skin has two faces: the grain, which is the outer, more compact part, and the inside or the flesh, which is more velvety. The flesh side is where the paring is done to facilitate the manipulation necessary for covering a book.

• **Goatskin**. This is the best quality leather, since the flesh side is compact and has a clear grain on the topside. It is sold in many colors and finishes, in natural or artificial grain. The kind most frequently used in bookbinding is chagrin, a high-quality leather with a fine grain and great flexibility. Morocco leather is also used. Traditionally from Morocco, this goatskin has a somewhat coarser grain. Today, morocco leather refers to all high-quality, natural-grain goatskins and is one of the most desirable leathers for artistic binding.

• **Lambskin or sheepskin**. These cured skins produce a soft, porous leather that's not very firm. It's economical for bookbinding and takes a great many finishes and colors, even though it's difficult to pare and emboss. It can be dyed with iron oxide to create arboreal shapes (Spanish-style). When wrinkled, it can also be veined or marbled with bright colors—usually red, green, blue, and brown (Valencian-style).

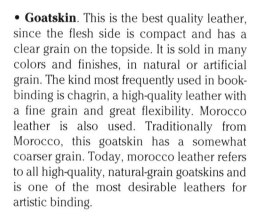

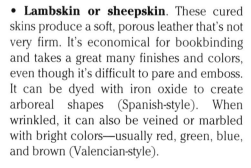

▲ Goatskin is the most commonly used leather in the workshop because of its texture and quality.

▲ Sheepskin in various mottled and dyed varieties was commonly used in the 18th century and is still used in modern bookbinding.

▼ Mull is a cotton fabric used to reinforce the spine and joints of a book.

▲ Parchment must be fine and thin to produce good work.

▲ Various shades of suede are generally used for making end sheets and lining slipcases.

▼ A set of basic items for gilding page edges: Armenian bole, egg glaire, and beeswax

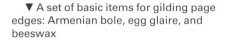

• **Calfskin**. This hide usually has a smooth surface and fine grain. In the early periods of bookmaking, it was very commonly used in bookbinding. Today, it's used in the restoration of antique books. Cured calfskin is often used in its natural color.

• **Parchment**. This material comes from the skin of a lamb, goat, or cow that has been cured with lime. The finest parchments are referred to as vellum. It is difficult to work, especially since it changes shape when exposed to changes in humidity.

• **Suede**. The velvety flesh side of this leather is used as the face of it. It is used mainly for lining end sheets, slipcases, and chemises.

Materials for Embossing and Gold Leaf

Gilding is a complex technique that requires special tools, especially gilding with gold leaf. Some bookbinders don't undertake this process, and allow professional gilders to take care of it. For gilding, the essential material is gold leaf—very thin sheets of pure gold with a tiny admixture of silver or copper that adds color and texture. To make gold leaf, an ingot is subjected to pressure through metal rollers until a fine strip of gold is produced that can be cut into small sheets. The sheets are alternated with thin paper and made into booklets with 25 sheets sold in packets of 20. Formerly, gold leaf was beaten out by hand, but today it's made on a machine, which produces comparable material.

Materials used to apply gold leaf vary, depending on whether you're applying it to leather covers or page edges. To apply it to leather, you'll use glaire, traditionally made of egg white. Today, you can use a synthetic glaire, which serves the same function.

You'll also need glaire for gilding the edges, such as egg glaire or food-grade gelatin. To provide gloss and color to the gold, apply a layer of reddish Armenian bole. Beeswax is used to facilitate burnishing and produce more shine.

Gold foil is another material used for gilding and gold stamping. It is composed of a plastic film on which gold is deposited, followed by a layer of heat-activated adhesive. Since it doesn't require any preparation, it's a very good choice for cloth, paper, plastic, and other difficult surfaces.

▼ Gold leaf is handled with a gold knife and a little cotton.

It's difficult to define an ideal bookbinding workshop, since they vary according to the jobs to be performed. Fortunately, bookbinding for single items can usually be done in small spaces. For example, such a workshop requires a much smaller space for the tasks needed than one accommodating the creation of portfolios for large graphic works.

Large craft workshops with many workers have faded into the past. Currently the largest number of people working together in a single company is around 10. But in most contemporary workshops, the bookbinder works alone.

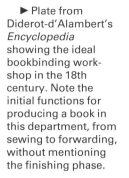

► Plate from Diderot-d'Alambert's *Encyclopedia* showing the ideal bookbinding workshop in the 18th century. Note the initial functions for producing a book in this department, from sewing to forwarding, without mentioning the finishing phase.

The Location

A binding workshop needs natural light because, once the works are finished, they will be viewed in natural sunlight. In addition, it should have good ventilation, since different kinds of adhesives are used.

Naturally, you'll need running water and a sink or washbasin for washing your hands carefully as well as doing the small restoration tasks that are necessary in many jobs.

It must be sufficiently large to allow us to move around freely. For that purpose the equipment, shelves, and workbench must be arranged conveniently so that one item doesn't interfere with the proper use of another.

Arranging the Materials

It's a good idea to keep small tools in a chest or on a shelf under the bench on which the work is usually performed, to keep them within reach and organized. Doing this will also help us keep your tabletop clutter-free.

Fabrics are usually kept on flat shelves, although, if you don't have room, they can be stored vertically to prevent damage to them. Leathers must be kept in a small closed closet to protect them from light. Roll them up, and never store them in a vertical position.

For gold tooling, it's ideal to have a separate table located far away from the dust produced by the workshop. Keep this table clean at all times. In general, tidiness is a basic requirement for bookbinding, but especially for gilding and gold tooling. Dust is the main enemy of the gilder who is working with glaire and gold leaf.

▼ Plate from the Diderot-d'Alambert *Encyclopedia* showing a bookbinding workshop in the final stage of book production: finishing and tooling. These two workshops were performing the tasks with quick efficiency as early as the 18th century.

▼ Drawing of a standing press from the 18th century. In contrast to modern hand-wheel-operated presses, the force is applied using a removable bar as a lever.

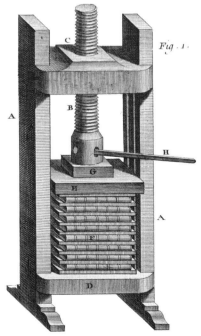

*B*ookbinding is used to dignify and protect a book for daily use. This chapter introduces various bookbinding processes and the variety of materials that you can use, such as fine fabrics or good papers. You can also use leather and parchment, which can be treated to produce different finishes.

In addition to securing the pages and attaching covers to protect them, the binder also finishes and embellishes the work. In doing this work, he must consider the weight, thickness of the signatures, paper quality, and other features of each volume. Thus, each book has individual requirements for each of the binding processes.

This section consists of two very different systems of binding: one for books with flexible covers that generally applies to simple or lightweight books, and one for hardcover bindings, such as leather, that is a more durable system. The two systems use similar procedures and, even though the results are different, each way lends equal dignity to the book's finish.

Bookbinding

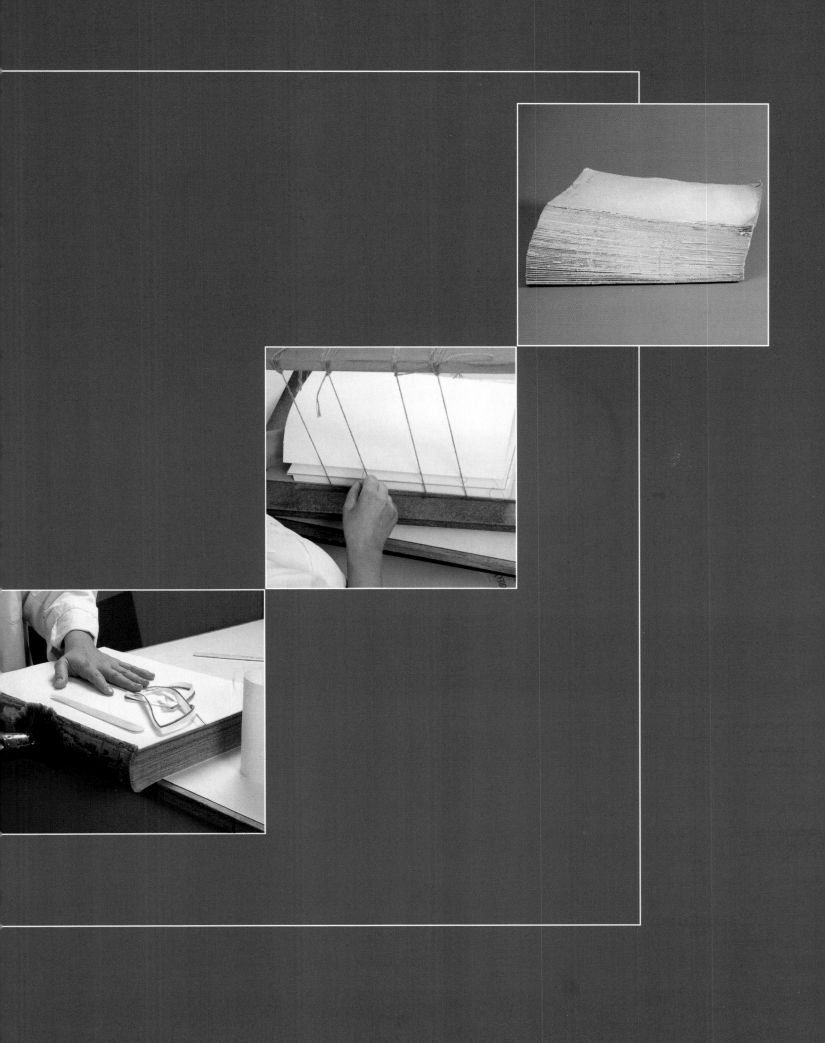

Parts of a Book

Back Corners
The corners at the inside head and tail of the cover boards are nicked to produce the back corners that facilitate the formation of the endcaps and the opening of the book.

Trimmed Head
The exposed top section of the textblock after trimming. In this example, it is gilded.

Corners
The outer corners of the cover when covered separately with leather, cloth, or some other material

Endcap
The head and tail of leather bindings formed to partially cover and protect the endbands

Title Label
A thin piece of leather or paper, often of a different color or tone than the rest of the binding, that shows the author, title, and, if applicable, the work's volume number.

Square
The space that extends from the edge of the pages to the board

Spine
The section of the cover that protects the signature folds and connects the front and back boards

Sides
Boards partially covered in different materials (paper, fabric, silk, etc.) on quarter- or half-leather bindings (see below)

Raised Bands
Ridges (often covered sewing supports) that protrude horizontally from the spine of leather-bound books. The space between two raised bands is called a panel.

Binding in Half and Quarter Leather
A half-leather binding is one in which only the spine and corners are covered in leather (as shown here). Quarter-leather bindings cover only the spine.

PEDRO MÁRTIR DE ANGLERIA

De Rebus Oceanis

BARCELONA 1924

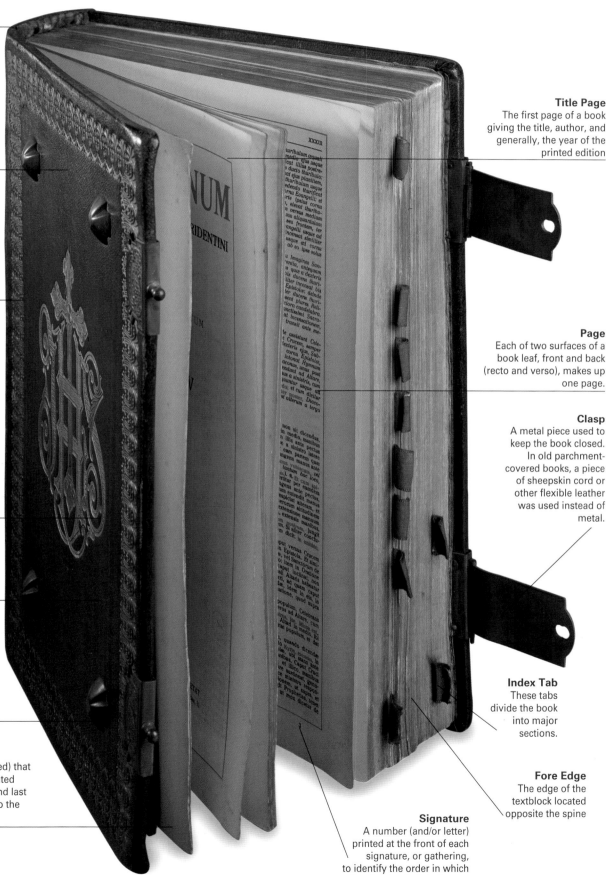

Endband
A sewn reinforcement and decoration, often of silk, that is located at the book's head and tail

Front and Back Covers
The front cover corresponds to the beginning of the book, and the back cover serves as the end of it.

Shoulders
The areas formed at the back edge of the outer signatures (see illustration on page 47). The cover boards fit against the shoulders.

Armorial Seal
Customarily found on earlier printed books, this embossed design on the front cover identified the book's owner.

Full Leather Binding
A binding covered totally in leather

Decorative and Protective Bosses
Ornaments and protective elements, usually of metal, found on larger books

End Sheets
Extra leaves (blank or decorated) that come before and after the printed pages in a binding. The first and last leaves are normally adhered to the inside of the covers.

Title Page
The first page of a book giving the title, author, and generally, the year of the printed edition

Page
Each of two surfaces of a book leaf, front and back (recto and verso), makes up one page.

Clasp
A metal piece used to keep the book closed. In old parchment-covered books, a piece of sheepskin cord or other flexible leather was used instead of metal.

Index Tab
These tabs divide the book into major sections.

Fore Edge
The edge of the textblock located opposite the spine

Signature
A number (and/or letter) printed at the front of each signature, or gathering, to identify the order in which the sheets of printed pages should be bound.

When you rebind a book, give it the same amount of care, whether the book is new or old, well or poorly sewn, in good or bad condition. To begin this process, disbind the signatures or trim the spine if the book is a single-leaf adhesive binding. As you do this, remove as much glue as possible to prepare the book for sewing.

A Clothbound Book

A Book of Signatures

In order to take apart this kind of book, begin by removing the covers. Take care to avoid damaging the first and last sheets to which the covers may be securely glued. If possible, preserve the spine as a reminder of what it contained when the book was printed. Next, prepare the book for disbinding by removing the old adhesive. Then proceed by cutting the threads of the original sewing, opening each signature right to the center and snipping the exposed thread. To avoid damaging the book, line up all the pages perfectly to form a compact block, then pull away each signature with your left hand while holding the rest of the book firmly with your right hand. The difficulty of this process depends on the type of adhesive originally used on the book.

Once you've finished the disbinding process, you'll have four pieces: the bookblock composed of signatures, the front cover, the spine, and the back cover. If any of these items is broken or in bad condition, restore it as explained in the paper restoration section later in this book.

• **Hinges**. Strong and flexible paper or Japanese tissue hinges allow the original paper covers to open properly upon reattachment to the text, even if the covers are fairly stiff. To readhere the original front and back paper covers onto the book, cut two strips of thin flexible paper or Japanese tissue the length of the book and about $1/2$ inch (1.3 cm) wide. For greater flexibility, make sure they're cut in the direction of the grain. At the inside edge of the front cover, apply a thin bead of adhesive (about $5/64$ inch [2 mm]), and attach it to the edge of a hinge. Allow about $3/8$ inch (9.5 mm) of the hinge to extend beyond the paper cover. Wrap this extension around the first and last signatures

at the backfold, and tip it onto the inside edge. Mount the original spine to paper or Japanese tissue slightly larger than the spine so the paper can be trimmed squarely after it dries, leaving a small flap on one side to be glued under the back cover after it's been hinged. When the bookblock is completely prepared, leave it in the press and consolidate the backfolds of the signatures.

A Book of Single Leaves

If the book is made up of individual pages, the hinges should be a bit narrower, since they won't have to go around the signatures and can be cut to the book's exact dimensions. Tip on the original paper covers to the hinges as described above. After aligning or jogging the pages together evenly at the spine, apply a thin coat of PVA to the spine before proceeding to the sawing.

Sawing

In the case of books made up of signatures or individual pages, take the steps above before proceeding to the sawing. Then cut out two pieces of binders' board about the same size as the book, and place them on the front and the back of the book. Align them with the bookblock and position them, spine up, in the lying press so that about $3/4$ inch (1.9 cm) of the spine sticks out.

With a fine-tooth saw, make a cut in the spine to the depth of the inside folio and of the signature(s), about $1/2$ inch (1.3 cm) from the top and $5/8$ inch (1.6 cm) from the bottom. Next, with a slightly coarser saw, make three more cuts across the spine: one precisely at the midpoint between the two previous ones, and the other two about a third of the way up from the outer ones to the middle one (see the illustration on page 40).

▲ Cutting the threads of the previous sewing and opening the signature as far as possible to avoid damaging the paper

▲ When removing the signature, support the book with your right hand while pulling with your left to make sure that the signature comes out as a single unit.

Sewing is an important part of bookbinding. Because the thread you'll use in the binding process isn't strong enough by itself to hold up to future handling of the book, it will have to be reinforced later. Eventually, we'll describe this step, but, for now, let's take a look at the types of thread that can be used for bookbinding:

• **Nylon thread.** This economical thread is very commonly used in commercial bookbinding, but it can also be used for binding by hand. Its main drawback is that it's made with synthetic fibers and is therefore slightly elastic, which can damage a signature that's not in good condition as it passes through it.

• **Hemp thread**. This thread is usually a bit thicker than linen thread.

• **Linen thread**. This thread is thinner than hemp thread.

Hemp and linen threads can be used interchangeably, depending on the thickness of the signature that you'll be sewing. When sewing signatures, the thread's thickness is important, since it must pass through one signature after another. For example, if you're sewing a book of thin signatures with a hemp thread of considerable thickness, the result can be a spine that's out of proportion to the front edge of the pages. When the spine is rounded, the swelling caused by the thick thread can make it too wide for the finishing processes.

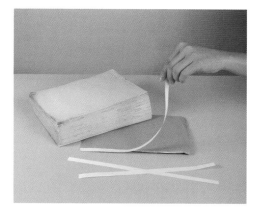

▲ Adhere the hinge $^5/_{64}$ to $^7/_{64}$ inch (2 to 3 mm) on the inner part of the cover.

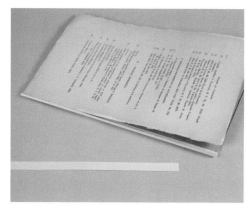

▲ Fold the hinge $^7/_{64}$ to $^5/_{32}$ inch (3 to 4 mm) from the cover so it can be glued to the inside of the folds of the first and last signature.

▲ Book prepared for sawing

▶ Sawing a book held between two boards

▼ Depending on the size of the book, it can be sewn with three, four, or more cords.

▶ Preparing the sewing frame and carefully matching up the cords to the saw cuts

Sewing "All Along"

This type of stitch should be done on a sewing frame to ensure good results. (It can be done without the frame, but the execution probably won't be as good.) To prepare the sewing frame, cut the cords longer than needed. Then tie the sewing keys or some pieces of cardboard to one end to secure to the lower part of the frame, under the slot. The cords should be under moderate tension and tied to the upper crossbeam.

Place the sawed book facedown on top of the sewing frame (see page 42) and adjust the cords so they match up with the three or more central saw-kerfs in the book. To finish applying tension to the cords, raise the crossbar until the cords are tight and perpendicular to the plane of the sewing frame. Place the book on your left, with the cover facing up, and thread the needle with about 4 1/2 feet (1.3 m) of thread.

First, open up the signature in the center, and use your left hand to place it on the base of the sewing frame so that it's aligned with the saw-kerfs for the cords. Using your right hand, pass the threaded needle through the first kettle-stitch hole, always from the outside toward the inside, while using your left hand to pass it from the inside toward the outside for the next hole. Next, pass the thread again toward the inside of the book, through the same hole but around the cord. Repeat this procedure until the first signature is completed. Pull on the thread, always in the same direction as the thread to avoid damaging the paper, and leave about 2 inches (5 cm) of thread hanging at the beginning of the stitch.

Next, take the second signature, still with your left hand, and place it on top of the signature that's already sewn. Using the needle, pass the thread from outside toward the inside through the kettle-stitch hole opposite the one of the previous signature, as indicated by the thread, and do the same as with the preceding signature, but in the opposite direction.

When you've finished the signature, pull on the thread so that it's firm. At this point, there are two ends of thread hanging out from the end of the signatures: the initial one, which you left hanging out approximately 2 inches (5 cm), and the one from the second signature. These two ends must be tied with a knot before you move on to the third signature, which will be tied to the second by means of a kettle stitch.

If you run out of thread or break it in the process of sewing, you'll have to tie on another piece to continue working. Normally, a weaver's knot is used to tie on another piece of thread, which is always made on the outside of the book, although it can subsequently slip inside. You can also tie the thread to the kettle stitch itself to avoid bulges inside the book.

When you sew the last signature, you must complete it with two knots before releasing the book from the sewing frame and loosening the cords from the crossbar. Once the cords are outside, pull them through, leaving a tail of about 3/4 inch (1.9 cm) hanging out of the book. Then, cut the same distance from the bottom. You can also sew two or more books simultaneously, and then trim the cords as described above.

▲ Securing the first two signatures with a kettle stitch

▲ "All along" sewing in which the thread passes inside the signature

▼ Sewing a book of signatures with an "all along" stitch. Each time you pass the needle through, only one signature is sewn.

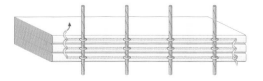

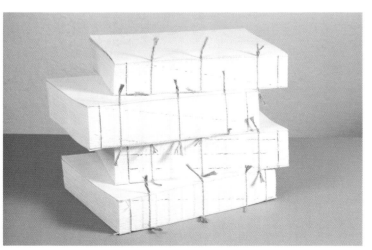

▲ When you work with more than one copy of a book on the sewing frame, the cord has to be slipped through the sewing so they can be cut apart at the appropriate distance.

◀ Books sewn together and ready for forwarding

Sewing "Two-on"

The main feature of this type of sewing is that it involves sewing two signatures with each pass of the thread. Using this system adds less thickness to the spine of the book than sewing "all along."

Begin this stitch in precisely the same way as sewing "all along," until you reach the third signature. Begin sewing it by going in through the chain stitch, going out through the first hole for the cord, and placing a marker in the center of the signature. Next, add a fourth signature and attach it by entering the hole that corresponds with the hole of the third signature that you just exited.

After exiting the next hole in signature four, enter the corresponding hole in the third signature. Repeat this pattern until you reach the kettle stitch. At the kettle stitch, proceed as previously explained, but this time, pass over the fourth signature, since every pass of the thread secures two signatures. When the last two or three signatures are done, sew them "all along."

"Dog-tooth" Oversewing

Once the single leaf book is glued up and sawn, separate the pages into sets of eight or so pages, depending on their thickness. Once separated, the pages form a sort of "signature," and you'll need to punch small holes in them for passing the thread through and attaching the cords.

Use an awl or even a small nail to make a hole next to the kettle-stitch position, near the edge of the book, and two holes on both sides of the saw cut where the cord will go. These holes have to be at a distance of $5/64$ to $7/64$ inch (2 to 3 mm) from the edge of the spine and the saw cut. If you leave less space, you might tear the paper when you pass the needle through (refer to the illustration). It is also helpful to punch the holes in the same direction that the needle will pass.

To sew, place the book on the left of the sewing table with the title page facing up. Turn over and lay out the first signature, holding it against the cords with your left hand, and pass the threaded needle through the first hole next to the kettle-stitch saw-kerf. Pull through and slip the thread into the kerf. Proceed to the first punched hole next to the first cord position. Pass the thread through

this hole, then whipstitch around the cord and pass the needle through the second punched hole next to the first cord position. Draw the thread through to the first punched hole near the second cord position, and repeat the whipstitch over the cord. Continue in this manner to the final kettle-stitch saw-kerf. Slip the thread through the kerf and then pass the needle through the punched hole. You can now proceed to the corresponding punched hole on the second "signature" and continue in the same way.

You cannot sew "two on" with this style of sewing. This method of sewing produces a tight opening, so if the blank inner margins of the printed text are too narrow, it won't be possible to sew it, and you'll have to opt for adhesive binding.

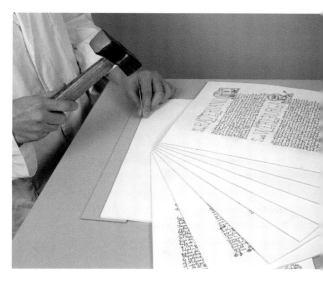

▲ Preparing a book of single pages for "dog-tooth" oversewing

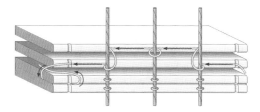

▼ Location of holes in a book of single pages prepared for "dog-tooth" oversewing

◄ Sewing a book of signatures "two on." In other words, every time that the thread makes a pass, you'll sew two signatures simultaneously.

► A weaver's knot, frequently used in sewing books because of its strength and the fact that it doesn't take up much space

Making a Sewing Frame for Home Use

A sewing frame is a basic bookbinding tool that you'll use often. Without it, it's difficult to secure the signatures properly and produce the correct tension in the cords.

A bookbinder doesn't always have a workshop large enough for storing all the tools needed for every operation. Since many bookbinders work in a small room in their home, they make a frame in a size that fits their particular space and needs. This frame can be taken apart quickly and stored if the space is needed for other purposes. For the sake of efficiency, the frame needs to be easy to take down and set up.

Use materials that are easy to find to make a frame. The measurements, given here, can be adapted to your needs.

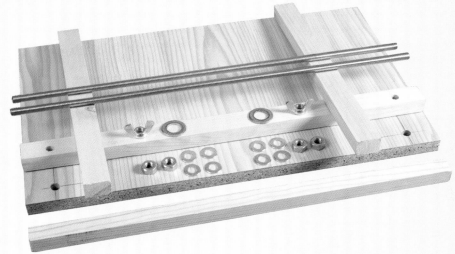

▲ **1.** Cut out a base that measures 12 x 20 inches (30 x 50 cm). Then cut a $^3/_4$ x $^3/_4$ inch (2 x 2 cm) wood lath the same length as the base or 20 inches (50 cm). Cut two $1^1/_4$ x $^3/_4$ inch laths (3.2 x 1.9 cm) to lengths of 13 inches and 20 inches (33 and 50.8 cm); the latter will serve as the crossbeam of the sewing frame. Use a hacksaw to cut two threaded $^5/_8$ inch (1.6 cm) rods about 20 inches long (50.8 cm). Once everything is ready, use a drill to make two holes in the base about $1^1/_2$ inches (3.8 cm) from the short edge and $^3/_4$ inch (1.9 cm) from the long edge, as shown in the photo. These holes serve as guides for the crossbeam, which you must drill to the same span but slightly off center width-wise on the lath. (Doing this will allow the crossbeam to be centered more directly above the sewing key slot).

▶ To make this sewing frame, you need a piece of veneered particleboard to serve as a base. The four cut strips are made of solid wood. These materials can be bought in practically any lumberyard, and the wood cut to order. To finish the frame, you need a threaded steel rod plus four nuts, two wing nuts, and the appropriate washers.

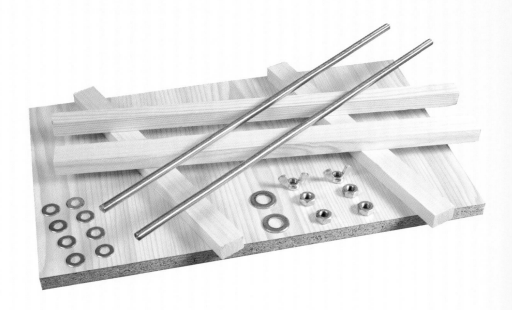

▼ **2.** Now you're ready to assemble the pieces. Nail or screw the 13-inch (33 cm) laths under the base about $2^1/2$ inches (6.4 cm) from the two sides and even with the back edge, with $1^1/2$ inches (3.8 cm) of wood sticking out at the front edge. Install the $3/4 \times 3/4$-inch (1.9 x 1.9 cm) lath there, leaving about a $3/8$ inch (9.5 mm) slot between the base and the lath.

▲ **3.** Here you can see how the threaded rod is attached through the wood of the base, with nuts on both sides, along with the appropriate washers. If you use a hacksaw to saw the metal rod, it's possible that the nuts won't thread on easily or at all. In that case, dress the ends with a metal file and eliminate any burrs left behind from sawing.

▶ **4.** Now, all that's left to do is to install the crossbeam on the upper part of the rods, placing one or two washers between the wing nuts and the wood lath to provide a more solid base and keep the wood from getting damaged over time. The holes were drilled slightly off- center in the crossbar because, once placed on the rods, it must be positioned directly over the sewing key slot so that the cords are perfectly perpendicular, top to bottom, once they're set up for sewing.

A Book with Single Leaves

Adhesive Binding

Once the book has been prepared, and before it is sawed or given a fine coat of glue, cut out some boards about 2 3/4 inches wide (7 cm) and as long as the book. Cut a strip of mull the same length and as wide as the book is thick (plus 1 1/2 inches [3.8 cm]). When everything is ready, the pages should be perfectly aligned before placing the pages spine up in the lying press, leaving at least 3 inches (7.6 cm) extending above the jaws of the press. Bend the pages over, fanning the back edges out before applying PVA with a brush. Bend in the other direction, and repeat this process. Place the book in a vertical position with respect to the press, and place the boards on each side of the book around 5/8 inch (1.6 cm) from the spine. Hold the book and boards with your left hand, and open the press to slide them down farther, leaving 1 to 2 inches (2.5 to 5 cm) sticking out of the top. Use the brush to spread out any excess glue, then perfectly center the mull on the book's spine and rub down with a bone folder. Allow the spine to dry down between bricks.

With this type of book it's a good idea to add the folio end sheets before gluing so you don't have to glue them on later. If end sheets aren't added, it's advisable to protect the front and back pages with a waste sheet that can be removed after the adhesive is dry.

The End Sheets, Fraying the Cords, and Gluing Up the Spine

The end sheets are white or colored papers placed at the beginning and the end of the book to protect it and attach it to the cover. To determine the size of the paper to cut out for the end sheets, cut the paper slightly wider than twice the width of the book and slightly taller than the height of the book. The paper grain must run in the direction of the height measurement.

Fold the papers in the middle, and make them fit the book exactly, cutting them with a board shear. Apply a 1/8-inch (3 mm) wide bead of PVA along the back fold of each end sheet, and attach them to the front and back of the book, aligning them carefully.

▲ Placing the book in the lying press with the spine up

▲ Fanning out the pages so the adhesive contacts each of them

Next, thin down the cords. To do this, pull the cord extension through the fraying board's notch. Then fray them out with a dull knife or awl point until the fibers are combed out smoothly. Repeat this procedure for each cord.

Use your thumb and index finger to spread the end-sheet frayed cord extensions into a fan shape, and flatten them down onto the end sheet. Next, place a small amount of paste on each extension, and rub them down to adhere them smoothly to the outside of the end sheets.

After the paste dries, place the book between two boards and make sure that it's jogged square in preparation for pasting up the spine. This time, you'll use hot glue or another reversible adhesive in case the book is taken apart or rebound later. Carefully remove the boards and let it dry, making sure that everything remains square.

▲ Once the gluing up is complete, lower the book between boards to within a short distance of the spine for applying the mull.

▲ When it's necessary to attach folio end sheets to more than one book, overlap the spine edges in a shingle pattern, guarding the upper one with a strip of wastepaper. Then glue them all at once.

◄ Once adhesive is applied, separate the end sheets for attachment to the bookblocks.

▲ Flatten the cords out with paste onto the end sheets.

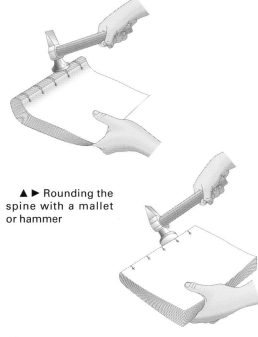

▲ ► Rounding the spine with a mallet or hammer

▼ Books with end sheets tipped on and cords frayed out

Once the book is glued up, it must be trimmed. Before you do this, take into account how dry the glue is. It shouldn't be sticky, but to work well, it shouldn't be completely dry. When it's trimmed, the book must stay perfectly square.

Using the Guillotine

If the margins of the book are even, place the book's spine against the *back gauge* of the guillotine without forcing it, and use the hand wheel to move the book backward and forward, trimming as little as possible off the front edge.

Once the fore edge is trimmed, round the book. To do this, hold the book by the fore edge with your left hand while using your right hand to gently strike the spine with a hammer from its center, then outward toward the shoulder. The signatures should move gradually and form a half-round shape. Do one side before turning it to do the other. Once the spine is rounded, check to see that the curve is uniform. If it isn't, adjust it with the hammer.

Trimming the Head and Tail

To cut the tail, place the head of the book against the *back gauge* of the guillotine and the fore edge against the side gauge. Position the spine so that the blade strikes this side first so as not to damage the fore edge. Trim the head in the same way.

Sometimes, because the spine swells or the paper is spongy, the guillotine clamp compresses the head and tail of the book, creating uneven swelling at the spine. To avoid this, you might need to pack the head or tail edge with pieces of binders' board before trimming. Place the board only up to the shoulder to allow the spine swelling to remain uncompressed when the clamp is brought down. Because impurities in binders' board can easily nick the blade, the board should be recessed so that it isn't trimmed along with the bookblock.

Some bibliophile editions are printed on handmade paper with deckled edges on the fore edge and bottom edge. In these cases, trim the book only at the head, and for reading, slit it open with a dull knife or a letter opener along the fore edge if necessary.

▼ Cut produced by a guillotine

Coloring or Speckling the Edges

▶ Items used in the speckling process

▼ **1.** For speckling the edges, you'll need a small screen and a stiff bristle brush moistened with aniline dye.

Water-based Aniline Dyes

Water-based aniline dyes are commonly used for coloring and speckling. Alcohol anilines aren't suited for this process. Dissolve the dye in water until it's the consistency you want, and check the color by using a bit of it on white paper with an artist's brush or a cotton swab.

Dip a damp piece of cotton in the dye without soaking it, and rub it over the edge, following the direction of the pages. If necessary, make two or three passes until you get a uniform result. When it's dry, polish the edge by vigorously rubbing a clean cotton ball or a soft cloth over the book's edges in the direction of the pages. You can also use beeswax for burnishing—apply a bit of wax on a cotton cloth or piece of leather and rub the edge in the same way, followed by a clean soft cloth.

You can also create a sheen by using an agate burnisher on the edges. However, if you do, the previously rounded front edge should be polished with very fine sandpaper before it's painted so that the "stepping" of the signatures isn't visible.

▶ **2.** Several colors can be applied to the same edge, but the brush must be cleaned every time the color is changed.

▶ **3.** During the process of coloring and speckling, try to keep large drops of color from falling onto the edge of the book. If this happens by accident, they'll be partially disguised by the variety of colors.

Speckling the Edges

To speckle the edges of the book, clamp it in the press in the same way that you did for coloring it. Have the prepared aniline dyes on hand, a small mesh screen with hatching about 3/16 inch (5 mm), and a stiff short-bristled brush. (You can also use a toothbrush.)

Carefully dip the brush in the color and brush it over the screen, allowing tiny droplets that are almost atomized to fall gently on the edges. If you wish to add more colors, repeat this process, adding hues that harmonize nicely with the previous speckling. Polish the edges as you would a colored edge.

If the paper is very porous, it will act as a blotter and wick the color toward the inside. To avoid this, prepare a very thin paste and apply it along the edges using a cotton cloth, making sure it's evenly distributed in small quantities so the pages don't stick together. The paste must be completely dry before you apply the colors.

Book edges can also be painted with other materials, depending on your ultimate goal, such as India ink and watercolors. Sometimes, motifs are painted on the edges that refer to the contents of the book or its decoration.

▼ **4.** Once coloring or speckling is complete, and the colors are dry, polish them with a cotton cloth or wax to give the book more protection.

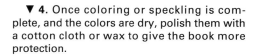

The shoulder is the projection formed along the outer spine edges produced by the swelling of the sewn signatures and subsequent backing. It provides board placement, protects against possible spine deformation, hides saw cuts and subsequent sewing of the book, and keeps the first and last pages from tearing.

To form the shoulder, use the lying press with beveled steel or wood backing boards, placing the spine in such a way that the shoulders extend beyond the backing boards the thickness of the cover board. This might be about $1/16$ inch, $7/64$ inch, or $5/32$ inch (1, 6, or 4 mm), depending on the thickness of the book. The shoulders must be exactly even on both sides of the book.

Once the book is in place, tighten the press and use a hammer to strike the spine at an angle from the center toward the outside so that the signatures spread. The backing must form shoulders at a 90° angle so they line up perfectly with the cover boards. When you finish the backing, try not to damage the end sheets, since these will be in direct contact with the backing boards and could get damaged by the hammer. Tap gently, especially when making the final blows. (With adhesive-bound books, there is no backing, and the spine is finished once they're trimmed and rounded.)

▶ This photo shows part of the process of backing the book. With the book clamped in the lying press at the right height, use the hammer to spread the signatures from the center toward the outside edge.

▲ Factory-made endbands in different colors

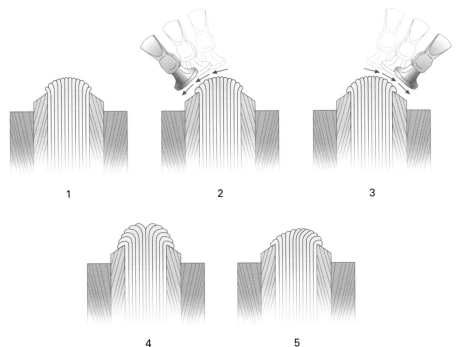

1   2   3

4   5

◀ The process of backing the book:
1. Place the book in the lying press at the desired height and clamp it tight.
2. Begin at the center of the spine, and strike toward the edge with the hammer.
3. Work from the center toward the other edge. Once the backing is complete, use the hammer with direct gentle blows to perfect the half-round shape.
4. Rounding the spine too much can cause defects.
5. A poorly shaped book can result in one with signatures leaning toward the same side.

How to Line the Spine of a Book

Spine linings are intended to strengthen and reinforce the sewing. For this purpose, you need endbands, mull, and a fairly strong paper to make what is called a "hollow tube" liner.

Gauze or light cloth about 1/2 inch wide (12 mm) is used to make the endbands. This material is connected to a cord of different colored thread along one edge. It strengthens the upper and lower ends of the spine and improves the book's appearance, providing decoration between the book spine and the cover.

You can use various types of adhesive to line the spine. It's a good idea to use reversible adhesives in case the book needs to be disassembled and rebound at another time. To the extent possible, you should also use pH neutral adhesives so they don't damage the book's paper.

Place the spine in such a way that it extends over the table's edge, making it possible to use a brush to coat the whole spine neatly with a thin layer of adhesive for attaching the endbands and the mull.

To attach the endbands, check to see if they have a front and back. Make sure that the right side is facing the spine. Adjust them with your finger and thumb, and use scissors to trim off where the first and last signatures end. The mull has to be the same length as the distance between the two endbands and shouldn't overlap them; otherwise bulges might mar the finish later on. The mull should as wide as the book thickness plus 1 5/8 inches (4.1 cm). Center it perfectly on the spine. Use a bone folder to rub it down and adhere it completely. When it's fairly dry, apply a second coat of glue over the entire length and width of it, and on the endbands to stiffen them up. Cut a piece of strong paper fairly wide that equals the height of the book.

The grain of this paper should run along the direction of the spine. It will have to be attached about 5/32 to 3/16 inch (4 to 5 mm) below the front shoulder edge and the length of the spine. Crease the paper at the back shoulder edge, and smooth it back over the spine so that it attaches near the front shoulder at the exposed adhesive. Rub it down with a bone folder to attach it securely. Cut or tear off the excess paper.

When this liner is attached to the cover, it prevents it from adhering directly to the spine of the book. This provides greater movement and ease in opening the book without damaging the spine of the binding. When you've finished putting on the spine linings, leave the book in a good position for drying.

▲ Applying glue to the spine for attaching the endbands and the mull

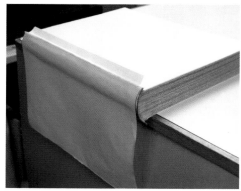

▲ Once the endband and the mull are attached, glue the spine again, placing the paper for the hollow tube lining about 1/16 inch (1.6 mm) from the edge.

▲ Completing the hollow

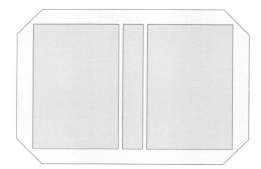

▲ Glue the boards to the fabric before cutting the four corners, as shown.

▶ Completed clothbound books

Making a Cloth Cover

A book cover is made using binders' board lined with bookbinding fabric. This cloth is usually cotton and is sized or has a paper backing to keep the glue from bleeding through and staining the outer face. Several thicknesses of binders' board can be used for making a cloth book cover, depending on the size and thickness of the book.

The grain in the boards for the covers must, as always, follow the direction of the spine. Use a board shear to cut the boards. First, get a square cut on your board. Then cut it to the height of the book plus $5/32$ to $1/4$ inch (4 to 6 mm), forming the square of the cover which extends over each edge of the book block. These dimensions will vary, depending on the book's size. The board mustn't be too big, but always a bit larger than the space that the endbands take up. Otherwise, they'll stick up above the covers and produce an unattractive finish. After the board is cut to the correct height, it must be cut to a width of $3/8$ to $3/4$ inch (1 to 1.9 cm) wider than the book. It can be trimmed to exact size later.

Trimming the Boards to Size

Position the boards at the front and back of the book. Adjust the boards so that the squares are even at the top and bottom and snug to the shoulders. Never trim the boards at the top or bottom, since that would ruin the parallel lines they form.

If the book was trimmed unevenly, it may be necessary to adjust (trim) the spine edge of the boards to make the top and bottom squares even and parallel. After this adjustment, if needed, you only need to trim the fore edge of the boards. With the boards snug to the shoulders, mark and trim the fore edge of the boards so that they line up exactly with the fore edge of the book block.

To cut out the spine strip, use cardstock or lightweight board, which are flexible and facilitate the curvature of the book cover spine. Cut the height the same as the measurement for the boards, and the width the same as that of the spine.

▲ Using a board shear to cut boards with the back and side gauge as a guide

▲ ▼ Various kinds of flexible covers made from papers in different colors and textures

▼ Books in half cloth with corner pieces that are correctly proportioned

Assembling the Cover

To record the board placement after final trimming, use a pencil to mark the boards on the inside (front/back), especially if they aren't perfectly square. Place them (board, spine strip, board) on the unpasted cloth with about 5/16 inch (8 mm) between them to check their position and measurements. The outside margin, or turn-in cloth, should extend about 3/4 inch (1.9 cm) beyond the board edges on all four sides. Make adjustments as needed.

To protect your workbench, use a waste sheet larger than the cloth that you'll paste. Use fairly thin adhesive that allows you more working time and helps the brush glide easily without leaving lumps. Spread the glue onto the cloth, from the middle out toward the edges, keeping it neat and evenly distributed. Place the first board carefully on the left part of the cloth so that the three margins around the edges are even. Place the spine strip at a distance of about 5/16 inch (8 mm) and centered perfectly with regard to the board's top and bottom. Next, place the second board in the same way.

Turning in the Cover

Pick up the cloth with the boards glued in place, and place it on a clean surface in preparation for cutting the corners. Cut the cloth at each corner at a 45° angle about one and a half board thicknesses away from the board corners.

Use your thumbs to turn the cloth in, always from the outside toward the inside, first along the top and bottom of the cover. Make sure that it is tight and free of air bubbles.

Use your thumbnail or a bone folder to "nick" the corners, and then turn in the sides just as you did at the head and tail.

Use the bone folder to rub down the turn-ins inside the cover, and use the palm of your hand to rub down the outside of the cover (a bone folder might cause shiny spots). This process finishes up the cover and helps assure total adhesion of the cloth.

There might be times when you'll have to use fabric that isn't commercially prepared for binding. But nearly all types of fabric can be adapted for binding if prepared correctly. They might even be quite thick and have a coarse weave.

To prepare fabric, back it with paper of the same size. To do this, apply an evenly spread coat of adhesive to the back of the paper. After you attach the cloth, leave the cloth and paper under light pressure, or give them a light squeeze in the press. Once it's dry, proceed as if you're dealing with a normal bookbinding cloth.

Fine fabrics such as silk, moiré, and others, or ones with an open weave such as gauze, are not good candidates for this preparation, since the adhesive will seep through the fabric if paper is glued to it.

To prepare this type of fabric, you'll need a piece of dressmaker's adhesive interfacing as well as a piece of paper cut to the same size as the cover cloth. Use an electric iron to attach the interfacing to the cloth, and once they're laminated, apply adhesive to the paper and attach it to the interfaced side of the cloth. Leave it under light pressure until it's dry.

SEQUENTIAL STEPS FOR BINDING WITH CLOTH

- Disbind the book.
- Clean and repair where necessary.
- Cut and attach the hinges to the paper covers.
- Saw the spine.
- Sew the signatures.
- Square up the spine and fray out the cord extensions.
- Cut and attach end sheets.
- Fan out the cord extensions and paste them to the end sheets.
- Glue up the spine.
- Trim the fore edge and round the spine.
- Trim the head and tail.
- Back the book.
- Apply adhesive and attach the endbands and mull.
- Apply adhesive and attach the hollow.
- Cut the boards.
- Cut the spine strip.
- Cut the cloth or paper for making covers.
- Apply adhesive to the cloth, attach the boards, and do turn-ins.
- Round the cover spine with the spine former.
- Glue up the hollow and attach the covers.
- Paste out the end sheets.
- Nip in the press.
- Inspect the end sheets.
- Leave the book under light pressure for 24 hours.

◄ Flexible cover bindings personalized with the initials of the library or their owner

Fitting on the Covers and Pasting out the End Sheets

When the cover is dry, round the spine strip of the cover using the spine former. Round it a little more than the book's spine. For that purpose, choose a groove that's narrower or more curved than the spine of the book.

Place the cover spine inside the concave of the spine former at an angle. Use the wooden, rounded-end dowel to work it into a curved shape, starting at one side and working toward the center, then working the spine toward the other side. Work slowly and press firmly to avoid making creases in the cover spine and create an even curve.

When the cover spine is rounded, use a brush to apply adhesive to the inside of the cover spine, not just to the spine strip, but also to the joint space next to the boards. Open the cover on your workbench, position the book on it, making the three squares even while leaving a little more margin on the front square.

Push down on the book with your left hand, draw the cover spine up onto the book by the front board. Do this firmly so there's no air left between the hollow and the spine strip. Once the front cover is placed down on the book, the squares can be adjusted, since the adhesive hasn't yet dried completely, and you can still manipulate the cover. Use the bone folder to rub down the grooves that the book forms at the outside joints, then set it aside with a weight on top until it's dry.

To glue down the end sheet, place the book on a piece of board that's smaller than the book; then, open the cover and apply a thin coat of PVA or paste to the outside end sheet. Close the cover and turn the book over, still on top of the wood, and do the same to the back part. Next, place the book between two boards larger than it, so that the spine sticks out from between them. Put the book with the boards into the press and give it hard, quick pressure for a moment. When you remove it from the press, verify that it is attached properly, and remove any adhesive that migh have squeezed out. Set the book aside between weighted boards, and allow it to dry.

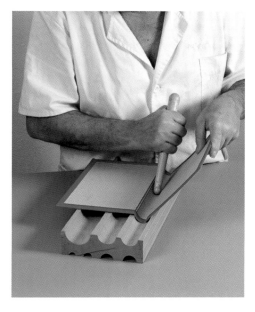

▲ 1. To round the cover spine, shape it in the appropriate groove in the spine former.

▲ 2. Position the cover on the book and make sure that they fit together perfectly. If space is left between spine strip and hollow, it will be more difficult to tool the title later.

◄ 3. Paste out the end sheets with a fairly liquid PVA or paste, always moving the brush from the center toward the outside.

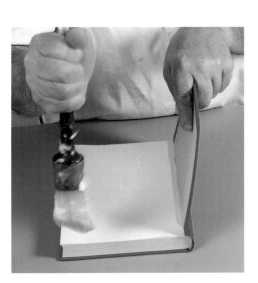

▼ 5. After checking the end sheets, return the book to the press or leave it lightly weighted until completely dry.

▶ 4. Once the end sheets are pasted down, position the book between two boards and place it in the press for a moment of quick, hard pressure. Check the end sheets for adhesive that may have squeezed out after the pressing.

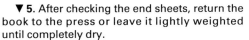

Bradel Cloth Bindings

These bindings originated in the 18th century when bindings were done in leather, vellum, and paper. Even though this binding was a temporary way to assemble books, the end results were beautiful and durable. Because of their simplicity and original style, they have become fashionable today. They can be decorated in an endless number of ways, from decorated paper to hot stamping, tooling, and onlays.

These bindings are easily recognized by a joint groove that allows the book to open nicely. Each binding is assembled in three pieces (the spine and two separate boards). These pieces allow you to play with colors or different materials, whether leather, cloth, vellum, or paper. In this chapter, we'll focus on the cloth Bradel, since this can be used as a point of departure for other materials. Next, you'll read about two variations of Bradel binding.

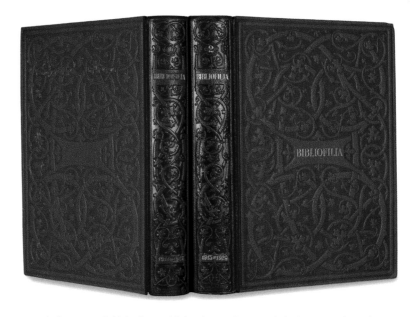

▲ Commercial binding with leather spines and cloth covers (1920)

One Method of Bradel Binding

Use this method to prepare the book as if cloth were being used, up to the point of making the covers. Cut the boards and spine strip as described for cloth binding. Next, cut the fabric for the spine the same length as the spine strip, plus about $3/4$ inch (1.9 cm) beyond the top and the bottom edge. Cut the width the same as the spine strip plus 1 inch (2.5 cm) on each side. Next, apply adhesive to the cloth and attach the spine strip in the center. Turn the cloth in at the top and bottom of the strip, leaving the sides free.

When it's dry, round it in the spine former. Attach the spine to the hollow of the book by adhering it completely, fitting it over the spine and down onto the end sheets.

Mount the boards separately on cloth, turning in the cloth on all four sides. To attach the covered boards to the book, paste out the end sheets and center the boards on them. Make certain that everything is lined up properly. With a quick pressing, this step is done.

When pasting out the end sheets, it's possible that you'll spread adhesive into the exposed cloth groove if you rush the process. Therefore, it's better to leave the groove area of the end sheets unpasted. Then brush a little adhesive onto the inside edge of the covered board where it meets the spine at the groove. Never glue the inside of the covered boards instead of pasting out the end sheet, since that will dirty the squares, and the covers will warp.

▼ With the cloth spine fitted over the book spine, it can be glued down onto the end sheets.

▼ Positioning the covered boards onto the pasted out end sheets

▼ Bindings with vellum spines and cloth covers

A Second Method of Bradel Binding

This second type of binding is perhaps more elegant than the previous one, and even though the finish is similar, the execution of it is very different. The book block is forwarded as if it were in cloth. You'll need two types of board for the covers: regular binders' board plus flexible, lightweight board, which will also serve as a spine strip. For the covers, cut pieces of both flexible, lightweight board and binders' board to the appropriate size (as described for cloth binding). Cut out the spine strip. Cut the cloth for the spine as explained in the first Bradel method. Paste out the cloth and center the spine strip. Attach the lightweight board pieces onto the cloth leaving 5/16-inch (8 mm) joints between the boards and the spine strip. Now turn in the cloth at the head and tail.

Cut out the cloth for the sides measured to the size of the boards plus 3/4-inch (1.9 cm) turn-ins on all four sides. Paste out the cloth and center the binders' board. Turn in the cloth only at the edge of the spine.

You'll end up with three pieces: one made up of the spine and two lightweight boards attached to it; and two others made up of the boards for the covers, on which the cloth is turned in only on one side. Now you're ready to assemble them. To do this, apply a thin layer of adhesive to the lightweight board and attach the cover boards in perfect alignment, with the turned-in edge toward the spine.

Next, put the cover in the press under light pressure until the glue dries. When the covers are dry and out of the press, glue up and turn in the remaining cloth margins on them.

The resulting combination of the binders' board and lightweight board on the covers is very durable, since the lightweight board serves to strengthen it and counteract the warping of the cloth. After the cover is done, put the book together in the usual way: forming the spine, attaching, and pasting down the end sheets. These two types of Bradel binding can be done with either a flat spine or a curved spine. In the former, use a piece of binders' board the same thickness as the one used for the covers, instead of lightweight board.

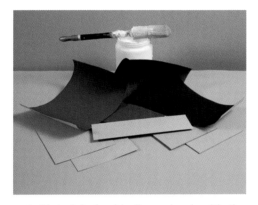

▲ Materials for binding a book with the second method of Bradel binding: two pieces of binders' board and lightweight board for the cover, the spine strip, plus the appropriate cloths

▼ Covered pieces of binder's board being attached on top of the lightweight board

▲ Attaching the lightweight board to the spine strip with the spine cloth

▼ Cover completed with the edges turned in, ready for attaching to the book

▼ Bradel binding in full leather with onlays by Germana Cavalcanti

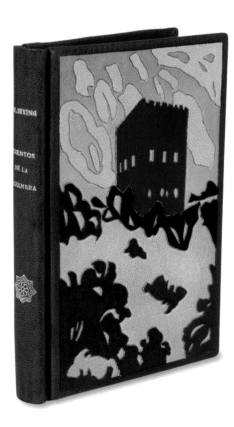

Vellum Bindings

Vellum is highly durable and was an inexpensive option for binding. Medieval antiphonals and books of hours were written by hand onto vellum leaves, then bound later in leather and tooled with gold. Thanks to the durability of vellum, there are still some copies of these books in libraries with titles inked on the spines.

These books were created in convents and monasteries for preservation and subsequent use and study. Several ways of binding these works are known, depending on the size and origin of the copy.

Vellum bindings were done relatively quickly, due to a reduced number of steps that were developed and perfected as time passed. It is worthwhile to be familiar with the whole binding process of this type of book, not only because of its historical importance, but also for practical reasons. Someday, you might need to restore or bind such a book.

Today, you can find books that are devoted exclusively to the different types of sewing used during that period. Here, we've limited the explanation to the most common methods.

Preparation and Sewing

To prepare for sewing, first place a double folio end sheet at the front and back of the signatures. Use hemp or linen thread for sewing; for sewing supports secure alum-tawed leather thongs to the sewing frame. You won't make saw-kerfs for recessed cord sewing, but rather do raised band sewing with the sewing supports forming ridges on the spine.

Set up the sewing frame in the usual way before you begin to sew the signatures. Since there are no saw-kerfs, pierce the sewing stations with a needle in the center of each signature and the end sheets. Sew in the usual manner, but wrap the thread around the sewing support instead of going over it. When you do this, a ridge will form on the spine that is larger or smaller depending on the size of the supports.

After the sewing is finished, use scissors to cut the sewing supports loose, leaving a tail of at least 2 inches (5 cm) per side for subsequent lacing to the cover.

Once the book is out of the sewing frame, trim it if necessary. This can be done right away, without gluing it, first on the fore edge and then on the top and the bottom.

▲ Sewing frame set up with alum-tawed leather supports for sewing

◄ 1. Sewing the endbands by hand

◄ 2. Once the lightweight board for the cover is prepared, the inward folds of the vellum can be unequal, depending on the edge.

▶ 3. To guide you in punching the covers with the awl, refer to the spacing of the alum-tawed leather used in the sewing.

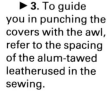

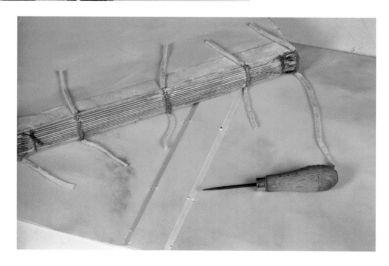

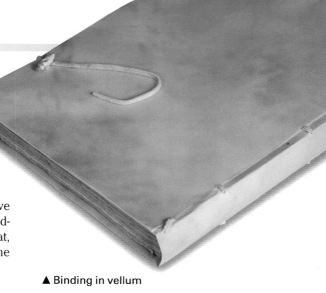

▲ Binding in vellum

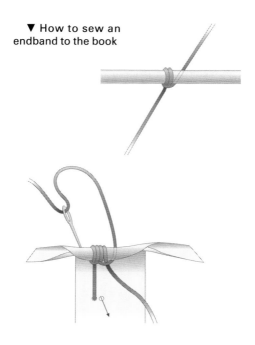

▼ How to sew an endband to the book

Making the Endbands

For this type of book, the endbands are commonly made of hemp or linen thread sewn directly in place. To make them, you'll need a strip of alum-tawed leather that forms the core over which the thread is wrapped.

First, attach the thread to the kettle stitch of the sewing at the first signature. Using your left hand to support the strip of alum-tawed leather at the spine edge, pull the thread toward and under it with the other hand, wrapping from the inside toward the outside. Once you've wrapped about 1/8 inch (3 mm), secure the core by forming a bead (reverse twist). Then pass the needle back through the center of the nearest signature and out at the kettle stitch. Repeat the process until it's finished.

At the end, tie the thread off at the last signature with a knot. When that's done, there will be several extensions of leather sticking out from each side of the spine. These are from the sewing and the endband. Don't trim them because they'll be used to hold on the covers.

Next, apply a thin layer of reversible adhesive to the spine, which will also give some substance and strength to the endbands. When that's dry, give it a second coat, and attach a paper reinforcement to the spine between the raised bands.

Preparing and Attaching the Covers

The covers can be made from binders' board or lightweight board, depending on the book's size and thickness. In some cases, the vellum alone can support the whole weight. If the covers are of binders' board, attach them as you would for a cloth cover, but leave a joint space of 3/8 to 1/2 inch (9.5 to 1.3 cm) between the spine and the boards. When lightweight board is used, cut a piece of vellum to the proper size and adhere the spine strip in the center. Next, you'll attach the boards. To do this, adhere the boards only at the spine and fore edge with a line of adhesive. Allow a 3/8-inch (9.5 mm) joint space between the spine strip and the boards. Turn in the edges of the vellum toward the inside of the cover to produce flexible vellum covers. The vellum must "float" on top of the lightweight board since it's attached only at the sides. If no boards at all are used, it's sufficient to turn the vellum in on itself. You must make four creases in the vellum cover: two from the inside that mark the edge of the spine strip, and two from the outside that mark the

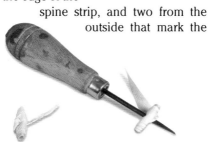

▲ Punching a vellum button with an awl

▼ Materials for making a vellum button and its closure for a cover

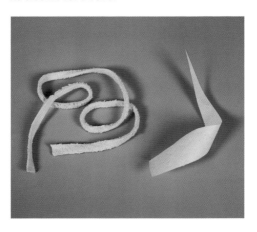

► A calligrapher adds the book titles, generally before permanently attaching the covers

joint space, or 3/8-inch (9.5 mm) away from the first creases.

Use a punch to make sets of two holes between the spine and the cover, corresponding to the number of sewing supports (including the endbands) of the book. Place one hole at the spine strip crease at the top of the shoulder and one at the crease near the bottom of the shoulder. After fitting the book into the cover, insert each sewing support extension out through the corresponding hole (top of shoulder), and then back in through the hole near the bottom of the shoulder before gluing the extensions on the inside.

Now the book and covers are a unit. The end sheets can be pasted down in the usual way. You can use a fastener at the fore edge of the covers made with a leather loop and leather or vellum bead.

*T*his type of binding lends a book more rigidity than a cloth binding. The process is similar to the previous one, but you'll add or change a few details as you develop the book's structure.

Preparing the End Leaves

Once the book is ready for sewing, and prior to sawing it, prepare four folded end leaves (with which you'll make two signatures of four pages each). These will be placed at the beginning and end of the book, constituting the extra pages that serve as a lead-in and protection for the book.

Cut two strips of linen about $5/8$ inch (1.6 cm) wide and the same length as the end leaves to serve as reinforcement. To attach the strips to the end leaves, apply a thin bead of PVA to two of the folios along the inside edges of the folds (where they'll be connected with the book). Tip on the strips so they extend out past the folds about $7/16$ to $1/2$ inch (1.1 to 1.3 cm). After they dry, set their matching folios next to them. Use a small brush to apply thin glue to the linen extension. Wrap it around the fold of the outer end leaf and down onto the outside.

You'll have two signatures of eight pages with a strip of linen glued on unevenly, that is, about $3/32$ inch (2 mm) on the part that touches the book and about $1/8$ inch (3 mm) on the outer part. These end leaves are temporary and provide the thickness of, or space needed for, permanent end sheets to be attached later. Consequently, it doesn't matter if the paper is blank or printed.

After they dry, use the board shear to trim the two signatures to the size of the book. Place them at the front and back of the book and proceed to sawing and sewing.

► Books that have been disbound, with signatures cleaned up, ready for binding

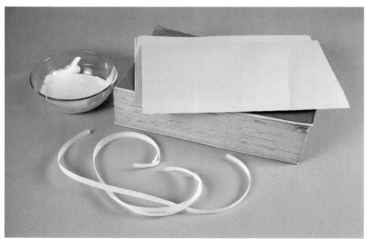

◄ Book with covers hinged and the end leaves prepared for reinforcing

▼ Preparing the end leaves

▼ Placing the false end sheets onto the linen strip

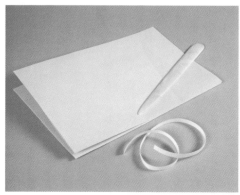

Now it's time to cut and prepare the boards. In our example, we're using a dense gray board in contrast to the lighter laminated board. You must calculate the thickness of the board in proportion to the book's size.

Use two boards for each cover. These boards will be laminated together, but you must keep a few things in mind when you do this. First, keep several thicknesses of board on hand and choose two different ones that, when laminated, make up the desired thickness for the cover. Cut them to a slightly larger size than the book, and then trim them later. Apply adhesive to the thinner one and attach it to the thicker one. Place it in the press for at least 12 hours. When you apply adhesive to a board, it will swell slightly and shrink when it dries, pulling against the other one and ending up slightly warped.

After the drying time is over, take the boards from the press and place them against the shoulders of the book. The shoulders must be the same thickness as the board or slightly greater, but never less. After backing the book, fit the boards to the book just as you would a clothbound book, but trim the fore edge square the same size or a tiny bit larger than the squares at the head and tail.

Place the slightly warped board, that is, the thinner board, next to the first and last pages of the book. When leather is applied to the cover, it will pull the boards in the opposite direction upon drying, minimizing final distortion and providing a stable, strong board.

Back Cornering and Beveling the Boards

Make an angled cut or nick at the top and bottom inside corners of the boards to help create the back corner and allow the binding to open better. This cut, shaped like an elongated triangle, can be made with a hobby knife or paring knife. The size of it must be proportional to the size of the book, since completing the endcaps later on will also depend on it.

Beveling the boards gives the book a cushioned feel after it's done. To bevel the boards, you'll sand them on each of their three sides corresponding to the three edges of the book. First, use a pair of metal dividers to mark out a line on the cover boards a little over 1/2 inch (1.3 cm) from the edge, except for the spine. Place a marked board on the edge of a fairly thick piece of binders' board along the table's edge to protect it from damage. Use a rasp to begin the beveling.

Next, use a sandpaper block to lightly sand down the three edges from the line drawn toward the edge, always working from the inside toward the outside, since the board is made up of very thin layers. If you sanded in the opposite direction, you'd create an uneven surface.

When you've finished, check the bevels to be sure they're even and the same. If not, touch them up and go over the cover with the bone folder to consolidate the sanded part.

▲ **1.** Laminating the boards

▼ **2.** Back cornering the boards

▼ **3.** Use a pair of metal dividers to mark a guideline for sanding the boards.

▼ **4.** Use a rasp to file down the edges, starting at the line.

▼ **5.** Final sanding with a piece of sandpaper

Attaching the Boards

Before you begin this process, make certain that the boards are trimmed perfectly to the book. If not, this is the time to correct this problem.

You'll need the following materials for attaching the boards: paste, newsprint or porous paper, a square, which could be replaced by a piece of cardboard cut at a right angle, a bone folder, and two clean boards for use in clamping the book in the press.

Use a brush or your finger to apply a thin layer of paste to the outside of the cover boards next to the spine without extending it as far as the tail or head. Next, position the boards correctly on the book. Use your fingers to smooth out the previously frayed cords and push them gently onto the paste on the boards.

Rub them down with a bone folder to assure perfect adhesion and distribution. Place folded newsprint on top of the pasted area so it extends beyond the pasted area on all four sides. After doing one side, carefully turn the book over and perform the same step on the other side.

When the book is put together, use the square on top of the table to make sure that the front and back boards line up perfectly. If not, adjust the covers since the paste is still wet. Next, carefully place the book between two boards and put it in the press, which must be tightened so that the cords blend well into the boards. Leave the book in the press for about 24 hours.

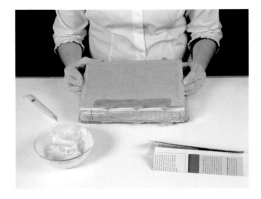

▲ 1. Applying the paste to the boards for attaching the frayed cords

▲ 2. Use the folder to smooth out any lumps in the cord on the cover panels.

FIBER DIRECTION IN LEATHER OR PARCHMENT

Even though vastly different from paper or board in most ways, leather and parchment have what can be called a grain direction.

It's helpful to keep this in mind when assembling a book, especially if it has raised bands, which will produce larger or smaller ridges in the spine.

On an animal hide, the direction of the grain follows the back along the spinal column. An animal reaches its maximum length when it is an adult, but it can gain and lose weight throughout its life. Since its hide is flexible and stretches, it does so perpendicular to the spinal column. For this reason, when a book has significant protuberances on its spine (raised bands), you should place the spine in the direction opposite that of the grain, that is, as if it were perpendicular to the animal's spine. As a result, the leather will stay secure on the book's spine.

▲ 3. Place newsprint or porous paper over the pasted cords, which must subsequently be placed in the press.

▼ 4. Books between boards, placed in the press, where they remain for 24 hours

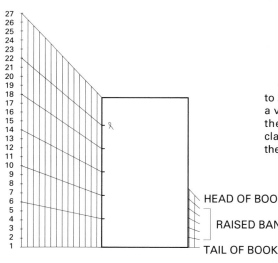

◄ If you divide any distance into 27 equal parts, beginning from a vanishing point, you can join the lines and thereby create the classic template for placement of the raised bands.

HEAD OF BOOK

RAISED BANDS

TAIL OF BOOK

Endbands are an important feature on certain books. They should incorporate colors that contrast with the ones used on the cover. If they're made by hand, they will be more aesthetically pleasing than the commercially produced ones. Many types of endbands have been made throughout history. Here, we'll discuss only two—leather and silk—since most others are derived from these.

▶ **1.** To make a leather endband, immerse a round cord of leather in a container of water for a couple of hours to soften it, so that you can work with it easily. (This cord will form the interior of the endband, which is called the core.)

▶ **2.** Next, place the core on a hard surface just at the edge of a piece of board. Use a bone folder to press it down firmly against the edge so that it takes on a triangular shape. Let it dry for a few minutes.

▲ **3.** Place the leather core on the top edge next to the spine in such a way that the right angle is aligned at the edge of the spine. Mark off the length of the endband.

◀ **4.** Use a hobby knife or a scalpel to trim the core where you marked it. Check the board once more against the book, just to be certain that it fits.

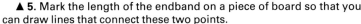

▲ **5.** Mark the length of the endband on a piece of board so that you can draw lines that connect these two points.

▶ **6.** In preparation for adding colored leather, use a pair of dividers to divide up the distance between the points so that you get an uneven number. You'll alternate the colors, and an uneven number assures the same color at both ends.

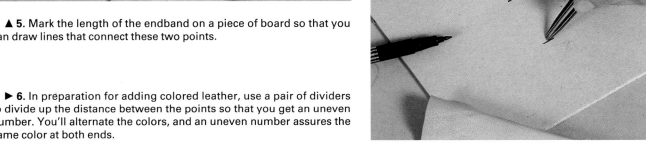

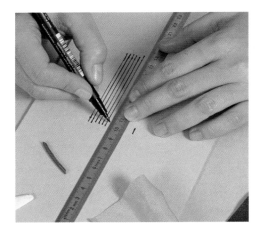

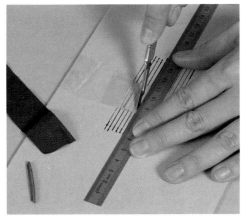

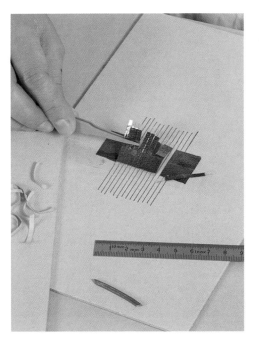

▲ **7.** Use a ruler and pencil to draw lines through the points that you marked off in the previous step. Make the lines parallel and equidistant. Since you're dealing with small intervals, take care to keep them even.

▲ **8.** Use a piece of tape to hold down a very thin piece of leather by both ends on top of the guidelines, allowing them to project from the top and bottom of the leather. Use a straight-edge as a guide to cut tiny strips of leather. Use a pair of tweezers to set them aside carefully.

▲ **9.** Repeat the same step with a different color of leather that contrasts with the first one.

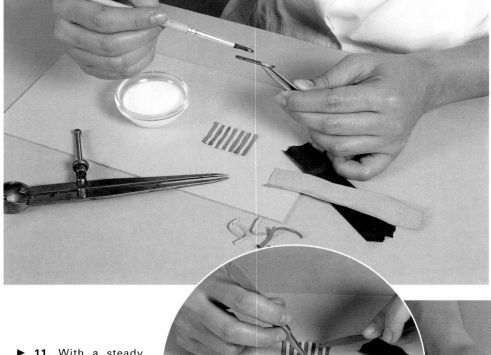

◄ **10.** Place the little strips of leather beside each other, alternating colors, until the desired width is achieved. Use tweezers to pick up the triangular leather core, and apply to the back of it with great care.

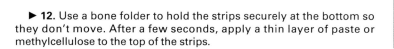

► **11.** With a steady hand, place the pasted side of the strip on top of the small strips of leather, making sure that they don't move and that they remain centered.

► **12.** Use a bone folder to hold the strips securely at the bottom so they don't move. After a few seconds, apply a thin layer of paste or methylcellulose to the top of the strips.

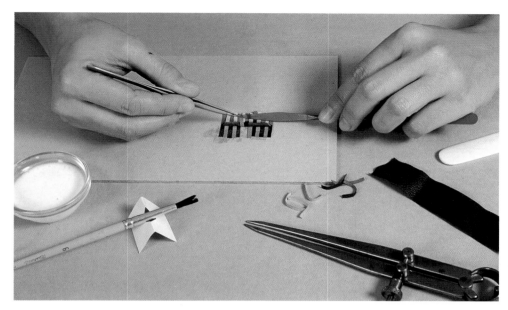

◄ 13. With the aid of tweezers and a small bone folder, pull up one of the leather strips and double it over the core so that it is pasted to itself.

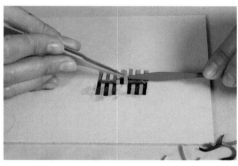

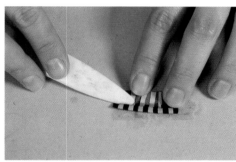

▲ 14. Repeat the previous step to fold over all the leather strips. If the paste dries during this process, just add more to moisten it.

▲ 15. Once the folding is complete, and while the leather is still moist, use a bone folder to tighten down the base of the endband.

▲ 16. When the endband is finished and dry, curve it slightly to fit it to the spine. This step must be done carefully so that the triangular shape isn't lost. It's a good idea to give it a little more curve than the spine shape so it fits well when adhered and won't pull away.

◄ 17. Apply a thin layer of PVA at the top and bottom of the spine so that it's easy to attach the endbands. Keep the endbands centered. Due to your previous calculations, the endbands should fit the book perfectly.

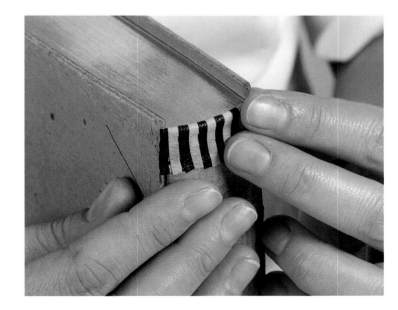

► 18. Once the leather endbands are attached, you can move on to the finishing stage.

Silk Endbands

This type of endband, like the leather one, eventually fits the exact dimensions of the book. Because of its characteristics, it is first made as a longer piece, and then cut to fit the book.

This endband is a more elaborate and attractive variation of what we saw on old parchment bindings. Commonly placed on books with laced-on boards, it is attached prior to covering them with leather.

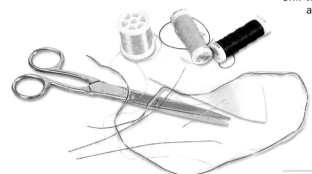

◄ Materials used to make silk endbands: silk thread, a piece of linen for use as a substrate, and two fine cords coated with a thin layer of adhesive to stiffen them before they're wrapped in Japanese tissue. The prepared cords form the interior of the endbands and are known as cores.

◄ Silk threads of various types and colors can be used to make endbands, but twisted silk thread is ideal. You can also use polyester thread, since the effect is very similar.

▲ Detail of how the endband is formed

▼ **1.** To make the endband, begin by threading a fine sewing needle with one of the silk threads. Pass it through the upper left end of the linen strip, about 1/8 inch (3 mm) from the edge. Do this from the outside toward the inside, that is, toward yourself, leaving a 1-inch (2.5 cm) tail.

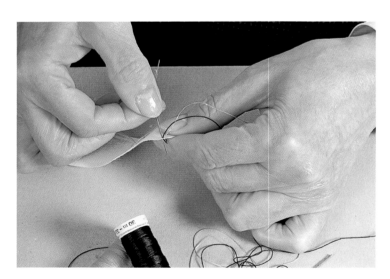

▲ **2.** Repeat this step as many times as there are threads, always passing through the same hole and from the outside toward the inside. When finished, knot all the threads together at the back of the strip so that they stay in place while making the endband.

► **3.** When everything is ready, place the cores at the same place as the knot, but on the other side of the strip. Use your non-sewing hand to hold the strip together with the knots and two cores. Allow one thread to extend out between the two cords, which is where we will begin, while the others remain hidden beneath them.

Take the thread held between the two cores and pass it under the lower one. Then, wrap it behind, out the middle, and up in front of the upper one. Without letting go of the thread at any time, wrap it behind the upper core and out through the middle, completing a figure-eight pattern.

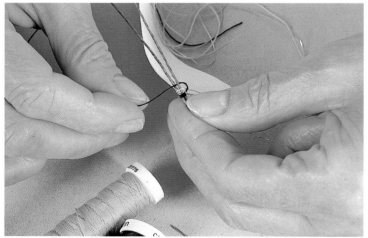

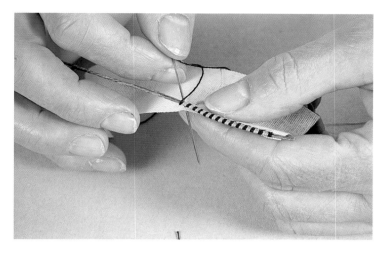

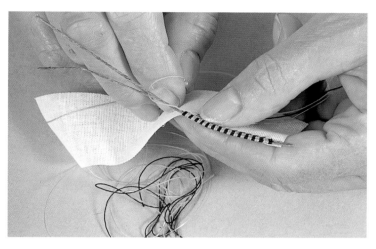

▲ **4.** You can use the same thread to make the second stitch, which must be passed underneath, behind, through the middle, and above the core before it turns and emerges through the center again. End that color by holding the thread straight down.

To change the color every two or three passes, take the next color thread and pass it over, catching the last one (being held straight down) at the base to form a bead. Bring the thread under the lower core, behind, through the center, down around the lower core, out the center and back around the upper core, repeating the initial step.

►**6.** When the endbanding is long enough, finish off the end with a knot or a bit of adhesive to keep it from coming undone. Be sure that it's sewn uniformly to the backside of the linen.

▼ **7.** To glue the endband to the spine, apply a thin layer of PVA to the head and tail of the spine so that you can attach an oversize length of the endband, extending past each shoulder. Make sure that the visible part of the endband fits on the spine so as to cover up any defects at the edge.

▲ **5.** One of the colored threads can still have a needle attached for anchoring the cores to the linen strip as it passes behind the lower core.

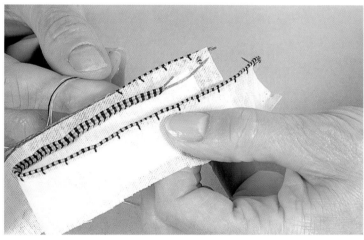

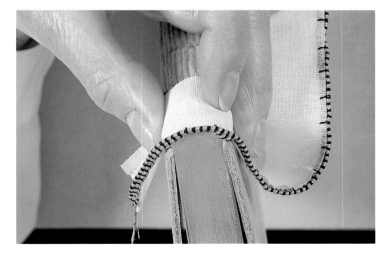

►**8.** Once the endbands are attached and all linings have been added to the spine, trim off the extra length from each endband. Thanks to the linings and adhesive, the band won't unravel. However, for insurance, put a little PVA at each end, which will dry clear.

Spine Linings

After a book that has been in the press (for board attachment) is dry, it's ready for lining. First, tear the newsprint off the cover boards with a quick pull, starting at the unglued part and moving toward the pasted one.

Next, brush some thin hot glue onto the spine, working from the center toward the ends. Avoid getting any glue on the head and tail edges of the book. At this point, the endbands are attached. The mull will be fitted between the two endbands and extend only the width of the spine.

To achieve this, cut the mull as long as the distance between the two endbands. Pull the mull over the glued spine between the endbands, and rub it down with a bone folder. Next, use scissors or a hobby knife to cut the portion of the cloth that extends beyond the edges of the spine.

Glue up the spine again and attach a paper lining. The paper should be the exact width of the spine and extend past the endbands.

Smoothing the Spine

When the glue is completely dry, move on to cleaning and smoothing the spine. To remove excess glue, pass a hobby knife along the shoulders, even with the surface of the cover boards. Clean the excess glue off the shoulders and from between the shoulders and inside board edges. Be careful not to cut the cords.

With a single motion, tear off the paper lining that extends past the endbands, and use a sanding block to gently sand the spine, always from the center toward the first and last signatures. By doing this, you'll smooth out any irregularities.

Lightweight Board for the Spine

After the front and back covers have been attached and the spine is smooth, it's time to cut the lightweight board for the spine. The leather will eventually be glued to this board. This board must be about $1/32$ to $5/64$ inch (.8 to 2 mm) longer than the cover and the same width as the spine.

Once the lightweight board strip is cut, use a block to sand down the two long edges. To do this, place the strip on top of a board, just even with the edge of the table. Sand the edge gently, about $1/4$ to $5/16$ inch (6 to 8 mm) outward from its edge, creating a slight bevel. Repeat this on the other edge.

▲ **1.** After you take the book from the press, and the newsprint has been torn off the cover boards, use the bone folder along the shoulders to finish fitting the book to the cover boards.

▲ **2.** Between endbands, line the spine with mull the exact width of the spine.

▲ **3.** Fit the paper lining to size by carefully tearing off the extra material.

▼ **5.** Use a hobby knife to clean up the inside edge of the cover boards.

▼ **6.** Smoothing the spine prior to the attachment of the lightweight board

▼ **4.** To strengthen it, firmly attach the lining to the endband.

Attaching the Lightweight Board Strip

Shape the strip in the spine former so that it's curved, and apply a bead of adhesive about $5/64$ inch (2 mm) wide, along both long edges, stopping about $5/32$ inch (4 mm) from each end. After applying the glue, attach the strip snugly to the spine while the book is held firmly in a press. Once it's in place, it should feel smooth and tight to touch.

When the book requires a perfectly shaped spine, add another piece of lightweight board over the first one. Use a slightly thinner board for this purpose. Once it has been shaped in the spine former, you can glue it right over the first one, and then sand it along the edges.

To attach this strip, carefully coat the first board with glue, since it's already in place. Then, center the second one on top, and burnish it down with a bone folder so there are no bubbles between the linings. Once the spine dries, go over it with the sanding block again to make the curve of the spine as even as possible.

Attaching the Bands

Use a template with a classic distribution to guide you when putting on the bands. Be aware that the placement of the bands affects the book's aesthetics, making it look heavier or lighter.

Decide on the arrangement of the bands, based on the type of binding and decoration you've selected. In planning the bands, keep the leather's elasticity in mind since it must mold over the raised bands. Thus, for a book on which you use five bands that are each $5/64$-inch (2 mm) high, the leather you use needs to stretch this much in order to fit.

Before placing the bands, pare the leather and stretch it. Then, place them according to the template using strips of board.

▲ **7.** Once the lightweight board for the spine is sanded and shaped, apply adhesive along the long edges only.

▲ **8.** Carefully fit the lightweight board to the spine.

▶ **9.** Attach the raised bands along previously marked lines.

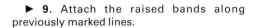

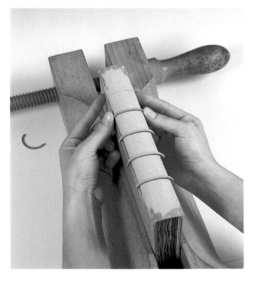

◀ **10.** Smooth the bands along the edges with a sanding block.

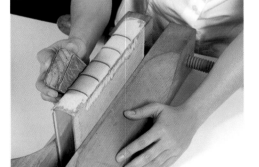

▶ A stack of books with bands already in place, followed by several books marked for placement

▲ Process of paring from right to left

◄ Leather pared along the edges and ready for paring the spine

Paring the Leather

Paring the leather with a paring knife reduces its thickness. Because the skins used in bookbinding aren't excessively thick, this process is done much like beveling, and only along the book's edges and spine. Paring is usually done on a slab of marble or even a thick piece of glass framed in wood that acts as a cushion on the table and keeps it from moving while you're working.

Hold the paring knife level, with the bevel facing up. Your aim is to slice the leather rather than scrape it, although this is sometimes unavoidable. Move it obliquely along the edge, keeping it at a slight angle.

Recently manufactured skins aren't difficult to pare. In contrast, skins that have hardened over time need to be softened. To do this, fold it so that the grain side touches itself. Use the palm of your hand to roll the leather back and forth in several directions, freshening the grain and softening the leather.

Commercial machines are made for thinning leather, but they aren't accessible to everyone because of their cost. The advan-tage of using them is that the leather suffers less than if thinned by hand, and the grain remains unaltered. In either case, however, you must manually do the finishing with the paring knife.

When a book is bound in full leather it needs to be pared about $1^1/8$ inches (3 cm) all the way around its perimeter. On the other hand, if it's bound in half leather, it should be pared only in the places where it's turned in and along the edges that are attached to the board.

Once the outer edges of the leather are pared, prepare the leather for the spine. This step requires mathematical precision so the book opens and closes perfectly. Measure the distance around the spine from the front to the back cover panel. You can use a piece of paper or lightweight board centered on the top and bottom of the leather to calculate this distance. Draw lines running up and down to define the area of the spine. Fold the leather back on itself on the drawn line, and gently sand it without damaging it or making any holes. Do one side first, and then the other. Pare the space created by these two grooves. Next, pare down the corners so they're very thin and turn in neatly when attached.

When the paring knife needs sharpening, always take it to a professional. Forget the idea of using a sharpening stone, or worse yet, emery cloth or sandpaper. But while you're doing the paring, you can run the paring knife over the stone in circular motions to keep it in good condition.

How to Mount the Leather

For books bound in half-leather, the leather shouldn't extend beyond a third of the cover width. If you have several volumes to assemble, first arrange the previously pared leather with the flesh side down in the order of covering. If raised bands are used, draw the leather lengthwise over the corner of a table to stretch it and facilitate its attachment over the raised bands.

Attach the leather spine pieces in groups of four. Do the largest one first and use fairly thick paste to paste them up. After pasting, fold them in the middle to let them soften and keep them from drying out too quickly.

▼ Process of paring from bottom to top, with the tool held continual-ly at an angle in relationship to the edge of the leather

▼ Use sandpaper to thin the leather at the joints.

Attaching the Leather to the Spine

Begin by unfolding the leather piece you pasted first. Coat it again lightly with paste, using an almost-dry brush to help spread it out evenly. Place the book with the spine facing up to place the leather, centering it carefully. Use the base of your thumb to pull the leather firmly down over the spine. Avoid stretching it so much that the grain begins to disappear. Once the leather is placed, use band nippers to lightly mark the raised band placement, and begin distributing the wet leather over the spine.

Turn-ins at the Head and Tail

To turn in the leather at the head and tail, place the book on a board, slightly open, and with the pages facing you. To facilitate turning in, gently pull the boards slightly away from the shoulders, then slightly pull the lightweight board back from the spine as well. If this step doesn't work on the first attempt, use a thin bone folder to assist. Turn in the leather smoothly and firmly, over the boards and the lightweight board, using the bone folder to rub down the turn-ins to adhere them as well as evenly distribute the leather.

As you attach leather to each book, stack them on a board with the spines alternating. After you've covered four, starting with the first book you covered, open each board all the way back, then push them forward so that the inside edges are even with the shoulders, stretching the leather slightly at the turn-in. Use the bone folder to assure adherence of the leather and smooth it at the board edges, then carefully close the board.

After you've set the joint for both boards, return it to a vertical position. Wrap a good, strong thread around your thumb, index, and middle finger, and pull the loop over the endcaps so that the thread sets into the back corners of the boards.

Slide the bone folder along the inside of the spine, pushing against the thread, in order to distribute the leather to each side and give it a harmonious curve.

▲ Pieces of leather that have been pasted up and folded in half

▲ Use band nippers for the initial forming of the raised bands.

▲ How to hold the leather for turning it in at the head and tail

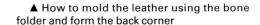

▲ How to mold the leather using the bone folder and form the back corner

◄ Lightweight board pulled around the spine to help form the endcap

▼ Finished book with the endcap and the two corresponding back corners clearly visible

The Back Corner and the Endcap

Use the bone folder to mark the back corner on the outside, and then make the endcap. Hold a strip of lightweight board around the head of the spine, even with the board edges. Use the bone folder to gently tap and smooth the endcap leather over 90° that extends past the strip, creating a straight base. Use the folder to pull out the ends of this "cap" and smooth it down so that it forms a half-moon shape. The same thickness should exist in the center of the "cap" as for the boards of the cover.

Now go over the raised bands a final time with the band nippers, to secure the leather and form neat, even bands. Place lightweight boards between the cover boards and outside pages. Then put the covered book between two pieces of binders' board underneath lightly weighted board to dry.

The back corner, a feature that lends elegance to the book, is the part that requires the most attention, since it's where the proper paring of the leather shows the most. If you're using light-colored leathers, use a fairly thick paste to keep it from softening too much, since moisture can leave stains.

Attaching the Corners

The height of the triangle formed by the corners, once finished, must equal the width of the leather extending onto the boards. Otherwise, you can use your own aesthetic judgment for establishing proportion. The spine leather must dry overnight before attaching the corners in order not to distort the endcaps while attaching them.

To begin attaching the corners, apply paste to four of them at the same time. Position them face-to-face in pairs so that the leather softens up. Apply a second coat of paste as you did to the leather, to moisten and distribute it, before attaching them to the boards.

With the cover open, attach the four corners. Position them so that the turn-ins extend past the board edge equally, that is, about $5/8$ inch (1.6 cm) on each side. Use your thumbs to fold them toward the inside without stretching them too much. Don't turn in the leather at the tips of the corners, but fold it together instead.

Next, cut a 45° angle through the folded leather from the board corner, removing the excess. With the aid of the bone folder, bring together the two turn-ins of the leather without overlapping them. After they're dry, finish each corner off with a small piece of pared leather that evens up the leather on the inside.

▲ 1. Attaching leather corners

▲ 2. Turning in the leather toward the inside of the covers

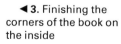

◀ 3. Finishing the corners of the book on the inside

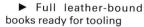

▶ Full leather-bound books ready for tooling

▲ Completed full leather bindings ready for tooling

► **1.** Placing the spine on the leather for an adhesive-bound book

Once you've applied paste to the leather, fold it in half and allow it to absorb moisture for about five minutes, then give it a second coat. Keep in mind that the moist leather is extremely delicate, and that any dirt on the table, your hands, or the tools you use for working will mar it. Thus, use extreme care. It's a good idea to work on a felt cloth while assembling the book and shake it out from time to time to get rid of any foreign matter.

Pull the leather over the spine, leaving about two-thirds of the board unattached. Proceed just as you did with the half-leather bound book—by distributing the leather on the spine and marking any raised bands with a band nipper. Once it's fitted to the spine, smooth the rest of the leather on the cover boards and adjust the position of the sides as needed.

Next, without opening the book too much, turn in the leather at the fore edge. Turn it in without stretching it. Keep in mind that the leather was laid out in advance, and any pulling at this point could damage the grain and spoil the finish. Once this step is complete, position the textblock vertically on a board with the boards open and continue with the head and tail turn-ins as previously explained. Leave setting the endcaps until last, since they could be damaged when you open the book to make the corners.

Lastly, insert the book into a lying press, between the felt, and finish nipping the raised bands. Once again, you need to place the lightweight board inside the boards and place it in a standing press between the felt and boards. The book must be kept in this position for a minimum of 24 hours to avoid subsequent warping.

How to Attach the Leather on Adhesive-bound Books

This type of book needs no cords for the sewing, and there's no need to attach the boards before covering them. For this reason, you'll mount the leather differently. After the book is trimmed, rounded, and backed, it will be ready for the boards, which have to be laminated together. They must be cut parallel to fit the head and tail of the book, including the squares.

Before using the board shears to trim the edge of the board that corresponds to the spine, square up the top or bottom of the board, and adjust the head to make sure that it's square with respect to the book. Now is the time to make any needed changes.

When everything is ready, cut the fore edge. To do this, fit the board to within about $5/64$ inch (2 mm) from the spine's edge, and use a pencil to mark the square on the front edge of the boards. The square should be the same measurement as the ones at the head and tail. Once you've cut out the boards that make up the covers, bevel and sand them in preparation for attaching them to the leather.

The lightweight board that makes up the spine strip needs to be a bit stiff. It should be as long as the pages plus about $5/64$ inch (2 mm), and as wide as the distance from one shoulder to the other.

If the book is made with raised bands, adhere them to the lightweight board spine strip, and trim them evenly. Once this is done, cut the leather (whether the book is half leather or full leather bound). Pare it on all four sides, and mark the position of the joints to the measurements of the lightweight board width plus about $1/32$ inch (.8 mm) at each side.

If the book is made without raised bands, the leather is ready for attaching. If raised bands are being used, you need to pare the spine and stretch it in preparation.

Once the leather is coated with paste and folded, and while you wait for it to soften, gently shape the lightweight board spine strip in the spine former without forcing it. Doing this breaks up the fibers so it adapts to the shape of the spine. When the leather is ready, center the lightweight board on it, and put the cover boards on both sides at a distance

of about $1/32$ to $5/64$ inch (.8 to 2 mm). Turn in the leather at the head and tail. If you're dealing with full leather, do the same at the fore edges and then finish the corners.

Next, glue the hollow spine of the textblock so it can be inserted into the cover. When the cover is still damp, it can be perfectly fitted. Because of the tackiness of the adhesive used to hold the spine in place, continue working on the spine in the same way as you would a binding with attached boards.

After the book dries, open it up to adhere the mull and attach the cover. Apply PVA directly to the mull, and gently fit it over the open boards. Because of the porous nature of the mull, and in order to keep the end pages from getting spotted, place a piece of waste paper between the mull and end sheets before gluing. From this point, proceed as if you're dealing with a conventional book.

▲ **2.** Placing the boards about $5/64$ inch (2 mm) from the spine strip

▲ **3.** Finishing the corners

▶ **4.** Nipping the raised bands with the cover open on the bench

▶ **5.** How to insert the book into the cover after rounding the spine

On books bound in quarter leather and half leather, the leather forms a ledge on the cover boards and has to be leveled before attaching the cloth or paper sides. To do this, use a hobby knife and straightedge to trim the edges of the leather on the boards so they will be straight, equal, and ready for filling in.

The fill-in can be made of paper or lightweight board, depending on the leather's thickness. Cut it a bit larger so it protrudes over the edges when butted up against the edge of the leather. When it's adhered into place and extending past the edges, use a hobby knife to remove the excess. Use a pair of dividers to mark the leather at the precise points where the cloth or the paper sides are to be mounted.

With the cover slightly open, place one point of the compass in the back corner that the board forms with the spine, and use the other point to mark up to the place where the sides will be mounted. This step is done at the head and tail of the book.

As we have already pointed out, the height of the triangle formed by the corner must be the same measurement as the leather that extends from the spine onto the boards. To facilitate this, use this measurement and multiply it by 1.41 (the square root of two), and obtain the length of the side of the corner. Use a compass to transfer this measurement to both sides of the corner.

Once you've taken the measurements and marked them, place a steel or aluminum straightedge between the marked-off points, and use considerable pressure to pass a hot burnisher over the projecting edge of the leather. This way, you'll succeed in producing a step in it, and it will be easy to set in the material to be attached to the sides. Pass the still-hot burnisher over the leather on the edges of the cover as well, reducing the thickness that can detract from the next step.

▲ Once the leather is attached, use a hobby knife to trim the edges.

▶ Fitting the lightweight board for filling in the sides

▼ The process of making a step in the leather with the aid of a straightedge and a burnisher

▼ Books bound in quarter leather

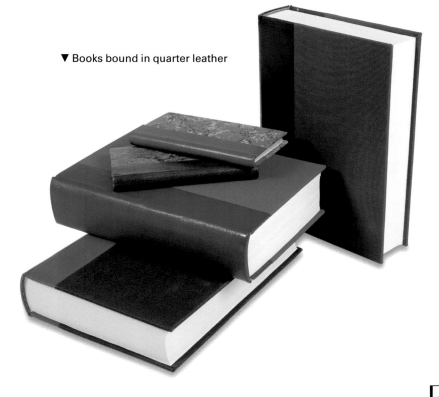

Attaching Paper or Cloth Sides

When you're working on a book that is quarter-bound in leather, it's very easy to attach paper or cloth sides. Simply cut the material by measuring it from the step produced by the burnisher, so you have an extra $5/8$ inch (1.6 cm) on the three sides (head, tail, and fore edge). Once the paper or cloth is cut, place wastepaper underneath it to protect the table from the adhesive you use to paste up the side pieces. Attach the sides carefully, and fit them into the step made by the burnisher. Do the turn-ins as if you're dealing with a book bound in cloth.

In the past, there was a custom of reinforcing books in quarter leather with tiny vellum tips. This is still done today. Cut some small rectangles of thin vellum measuring about $5/8$ x 1 $1/8$ inch (1.6 x 2.9 cm), and glue them on with PVA or paste. Next, attach them to the corners. Once they dry, pound them with a hammer until their surface blends into the board perfectly.

If you add vellum tips, you'll have to prepare the sides for attachment by cutting the corners about $5/64$ to $1/8$ inch (2 to 3 mm) toward the inside of the board corner so that, when attached, the vellum tips protrude slightly.

Cutting the sides for a book half-bound in leather requires more attention to detail, since measurements must be exact. Cut the material for the sides to the same size as for a book quarter-bound in leather. Then, fit it into the step in the leather formed by the burnisher on the side, and slide it up or down so as to extend beyond the board equally over the three sides. Hold it in place, then fold the corners back on themselves so they match up with the cuts for trimming the leather corners.

Next, hold the paper or cloth that you wish to attach so that it doesn't move, and use scissors to make cuts perpendicular to the fold at the points where the trimmed edge of the leather corners turn over the board edges. Use a hobby knife to make a cut joining the two previous cuts along the fold, then discard the cut-off portion. You can also use a straightedge to help with this task.

When you paste up and attach the trimmed sides and turn in the edges to the inside of the cover, notice that the corners are held in place as if by tweezers. This gives them a special finish. Keep in mind that it's necessary to center all the material perfectly. To facilitate placement, use a pencil to mark the edge of the side that joins the leather on the spine at both the top and bottom edge of the boards.

▲ **1.** Cuts made for perfect placement of the sides

▲**2.** Paper sides cut out and ready for attachment

▲**3.** Placement of the sides on the book covers

▲ **4.** Close-up of the paper inside the cover so you can see how it's finished off

◀ Finished books bound in half leather, ready for polishing and tooling

Board Linings and Joints
Board Linings

Lightweight board and paper, like moist leather, contract when they dry. Once book covers are dry, they tend to warp outward. To counteract this tendency, you must attach linings on the inside. Linings are nothing more than papers that swell with the effect of the moist adhesive. When these papers shrink back to normal after drying, they contract on the cover and counteract any opposing warping.

In the three types of binding already described, mark an even margin on the inside of the cover boards along the head, tail, and fore edge with a pair of dividers. Use a straightedge and hobby knife to cut along the marked lines and remove the excess turn-in material.

Next, from strong paper that's not too thick, cut a piece the same height but a bit less than the width of the area inside the cover board within the turn-ins. The width dimension will allow the paper to expand when pasted up and fill the area in both directions. (Apply a coat of paste to each piece of paper, and place the pasted faces together so they don't dry out from the air and expand as much as possible.)

After a reasonable amount of time, separate them and attach them inside the cover, fitted to the edges of the trimmed turn-ins. Insert a piece of lightweight board between the lining and end sheets, and place the book between boards in the standing press for 24 hours.

After this step, the covers of a book in quarter leather and a book in half leather will be completely straight. In comparison, a book in full leather ends up warping slightly because the leather stretches more than other materials and then contracts proportionally. In this case, you must use a second liner, which is cut and attached in the same way. If it seems that the second one would pull too much, use glue instead of paste to reduce the expansion effect.

▼ 1. Once the paste is applied, place the paper linings together, face-to-face, to maximize expansion.

▼ 2. Setting the linings inside the cover

Leather and Cloth Joints

Joints, placed inside the cover next to the shoulders, serve to embellish the book. They also increase the strength of the binding.

When a book is made in full leather, leather joints are made from the same material. Leather can also be used to make this feature on a book in half leather, although it's more common to use cloth for economic reasons. The leather or cloth intended for the joint should have the same height as the leaves of the book; the width, on the other hand, will vary depending on the shoulder and the thickness of the boards. The joint should extend about 5/8 inch (1.6 cm) over the inside cover and the shoulder, and about 3/16 inch (5 mm) over the inside edge of the end leaves.

Leather Joints

To make a leather joint, use the same leather that you used for covering. You must thin it down to almost nothing before using it. First, remove the bound-in waste sheets. Next, remove leftover adhesive from the inside edges of the cover boards and the inner joint.

Attach each joint with paste, fitting it at the head and tail to the inside shoulders of the book, and trimming it to size if it stretches after pasting. Use your thumbs to press down each joint at the shoulders. Before putting them down on the inside cover, trim the ends to a 45° angle.

Once everything is in place, leave the book open for an hour to dry in order to avoid wrinkles. When you've done this to each side, attach the linings on the inside covers, close the boards, and leave it in the press until it's completely dry. If you do this, you'll be able to open it with ease and without strain. On a full leather-bound book, the joints have to be attached after the first lining is attached.

Cloth Joints

The color of this joint should be the same as the cloth on the outside or a color that contrasts with the leather on the spine. Apply PVA or hot glue to a cloth joint the same way you'd apply paste on a leather joint. Also, place it in the press for several hours before attaching the doublures.

▼ 1. Mitering the ends of the leather joint

▼ 2. Rubbing down the joint

Paper End Sheets

The paper that you choose for the end sheets can vary from good laid paper to hand-marbled paper. Always attach them in one of two ways, based on whether the book has leather/cloth joints or requires a one-piece end sheet.

One-piece End Sheet

First, remove the bound-in waste sheets and clean up the spine area. Cut the end sheet paper slightly taller than the height and about 3/8 inch (9.5 mm) longer than twice the book width, depending on the thickness of the shoulder. When everything is ready, make a template from a lightweight board the same height as the leaves of the book minus about 1/32 to 5/64 inch (.8 to 2 mm) and the same width as the cover.

The procedure is simple: position the template at one end of the end sheet and center it top and bottom. Then, use a hobby knife to cut the paper to the template's height size; two 'steps' will thereby be visible at the middle between the trimmed and untrimmed half of the end sheet. Repeat this step on the other sheet.

Once the end sheets are cut out, they will have to be glued up. Apply glue only to the trimmed side of the end sheet plus 3/8 inch (9.5 mm) on the untrimmed side. Use fairly thin, hot glue because it dries quickly.

After gluing the end sheet, and with the book open and the open board supported, set the trimmed side of the paper on the open board so the three squares are equal. Use your thumb to press down the paper in the joint area, leaving the portion of the end sheet that touches the textblock temporarily unglued. Repeat this step for the other sheet, and allow them to dry open for a few minutes so it doesn't wrinkle when the book is closed. After closing the boards, open them again to apply a thin layer of hot glue to the blank page adjacent to the unglued sheet to form a lamination.

Next, set the lightweight board inside the closed covers and leave it in the press for 24 hours. Remove it from the press without removing the lightweight board from inside. Use a hobby knife to trim the end sheets to the size of the book against the board. Do this carefully to avoid damaging the edges. Be especially cautious if the edges are gilt, since they're easy to scratch.

Two-piece End Sheet

This type of end sheet is used when the joint is leather or cloth. Make a template for the doublure. For this, use a piece of lightweight board the same height as the leaves of the book minus 1/32 to 5/64 inch (.8 to 2 mm). To calculate the width, set the lightweight board on the cover leaving space for the three squares. At the joint edge, mark off the same distance as the squares, or a little more for the expansion of the paper, and then cut the width.

Having cut the doublure using the template, glue it up and fit it evenly inside the board. Smooth the paper with the palm of your hand to be sure it's attached securely.

The end sheet (flyleaf) that is attached to the book has to be cut 3/8 inch (9.5 mm) larger than the pages on each side. Next, apply a 3/8-inch (9.5 mm) strip of glue to the paper along the joint edge, and attach it at the base of the shoulder.

When it's dry, glue it to the blank page in the front and the back, just as you would on a one-piece end sheet. As a final step, put the book in the press, and trim the sheets to the precise size after they are fully dry.

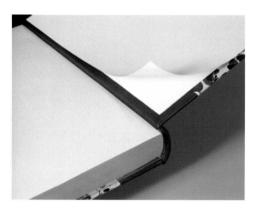

▲ Attaching the doublure of a two-piece end sheet

▲ Two-colored, two-piece end sheet with a leather joint

◄ Completed book with a two-color end sheet

▲ One-piece end sheet using the same paper as the sides

► Hand-marbled end sheet for a full leather-bound book

End Sheets in Suede or Leather

To make this type of end sheet, you must plan in advance to slightly modify the way the book is put together. Just as with paper, end sheets made from suede or leather can be made of one piece or two pieces, but leather ones are most often made in two pieces.

One-piece End Sheets

When you prepare the book for sewing, attach a piece of lightweight board instead of two false end sheets, allowing for the thickness of the suede. From this point, continue as previously described until it is time to pare the cover leather. Pare it only at the corners and the area near the endcaps, leaving the turn-ins full thickness. If you use thick hides, they'll have to be split to a thickness of about $1/32$ inch (.8 mm).

Once the book is put together, use a pair of dividers, a straightedge, and a hobby knife to trim out the inside of the boards to within about $5/32$ to $3/16$ inch (4 to 5 mm) from the three edges of the cover boards. Due to the thickness of the leather, you'll see a depression where the suede will fit. When you attach the linings, in addition to attaching the customary lining, you must attach a second one that fits the depression exactly.

Cut the suede the same way as the paper end sheets, with the trimmed end cut exactly to the size of the depression on the inside boards. The adhesive is a mixture of methyl-cellulose and PVA. To check the glue's consistency, insert an artist's brush into it and see if it drips slowly when taken out.

Apply a layer of this glue to both the suede doublure that will be glued to the cover and the lining on the inside of the cover. Doing this keeps it from drying too quickly, since you need a certain amount of time to fit the suede to the edges of the leather. Never force it, or you might stretch it too much or create wrinkles. Do this step without rushing. Also, make sure that your hands are clean, since you won't be able to disguise a spot of glue on the suede.

Once the pastedown is set and you've put down the joint with your thumb, allow it to dry somewhat, then press it closed with a lightweight board inside the cover boards. When this is dry, attach the suede flyleaves as described for the paper flyleaves. As always, place a lightweight board inside the cover boards, and let it dry in the press until the following morning.

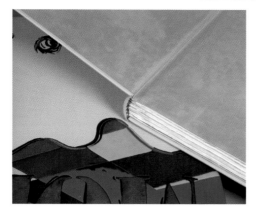
▲ Close-up of a joint with a suede end sheet

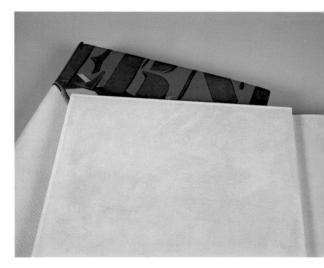
▲ One-piece suede end sheet

◄ Close-up of a leather end sheet: the gold tooling covers up the joint between the end sheet and the leather of the cover.

▼ Leather end sheet with gold tooling

◄ End sheets that combine leather and suede

▲ A leather end sheet that contrasts with a silk one

Two-piece End Sheets

In the case of two-piece end sheets, prepare the book for sewing with the same steps that you'd use for a one-piece suede end sheet, up to the point of laminating the boards. In this section, we'll explain the remaining steps.

After the book is rounded and backed, it's time to get the boards ready. This time, you'll use three: a thick board appropriate for the size of the book and two lightweight boards. Cut the boards about $3/8$ inch (9.5 mm) larger on each side than the book, and laminate one thin board to the binders' board.

Use a pair of dividers to mark the four sides of the lightweight board with a line about an inch (2.5 cm) from the edge. Very carefully, apply PVA with a brush to this outer area, then apply it to the other light-weight board. Leave it in the press until it's dry.

Once book measurements are made, trim the boards. Be sure to trim them evenly since

there is an unlaminated area on the inside. In other words, if you cut $1/4$ inch (6 mm) from the top, cut the same amount off the bottom, and so forth. Cover the book in the usual way. Because of the unlaminated area inside the cover, you can't trim out and line the boards at this point.

Pare and attach the leather joints as previously described. Attach a piece of paper the same thickness as the joint at the inside edge of it near the shoulder to fill in and make it flush. The turn-ins and leather joints can be cleaned with vinegar and then polished with a burnisher.

Use a pair of dividers to mark off a line about $5/32$ inch (4 mm) from the inside edges of the cover boards. Cut down to the depth of the second lightweight board along this line. Make this cut very precise. It's better to go over it with the hobby knife several times than use force and have the knife go off course and produce a crooked line, which would spoil the appearance and finish of the book.

Use the hobby knife to make two diagonal cuts inside the cover to assist in removing this inside piece. Do this bit by bit, moving from the center to the sides, since there are still areas where the lightweight board is glued down, or where the cut is not deep enough. If you pull too quickly, you can damage the edges of the cover.

Once the lightweight board piece has been removed, clean any remains of the glue and cardboard from the inside. The surface must be completely flat and smooth, ready for attaching the linings. For that, as with the one-piece style, you must attach a second lining as well as the first one on the inside of the cover.

The suede or leather doublure must be cut to the same dimensions as the depression on the inside of the board. Since you must take the possible expansion of the material into consideration, it can be cut slightly smaller. It's preferable to work a bit harder to get it to fit inside than to try to stretch it and fall short of the edges.

Put adhesive on both the doublure and inside board lining (as with the one-piece style), then set it in place and rub it down gently.

Attach the flyleaves by cutting them to the size of the book. Remove the fill-in and glue them to the extra blank pages, setting it securely against the leather joint edge.

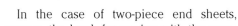

◄ Different types of suede for making end sheets

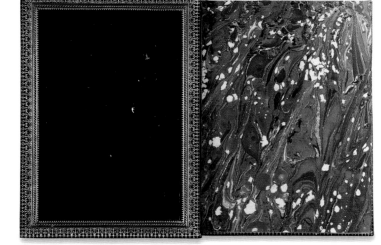

►End sheet of suede and paper

One-piece End Sheet

The book that we're describing is assembled in full leather until it's time to attach the end sheets. Depending on the type of material being used, whether silk or some other type of fabric, you'll anticipate the thickness when you attach the waste sheet or a piece of lightweight board before sewing.

Use great caution when installing this kind of end sheet, since it's impossible to disguise imperfections. Avoid having to repeat the whole installation because of a simple glue spot or defective binding.

The type of silk or fabric that you choose must harmonize with the outside leather and subsequent decoration. For that reason, cut the material the same dimensions as the open book, plus about $3/8$ to $6/8$ inch (9.5 mm to 2.1 cm) extra on all four sides. When you do this, keep the dimensions of the shoulder in mind. You can't apply glue directly to this type of material because it will bleed through and make spots on the front. (Although the material could be prepared for gluing by backing it, there is still a possibility that the cut edges would fray, and it would also look too stiff.)

Once the silk is ready and ironed, place it aside while you cut out the templates over which the silk will be mounted. Cut a piece of stiff paper the same size as the cover, minus about $5/32$ inch (4 mm) on each of the three sides corresponding to the edges of the book. This template will be placed on top of the silk about $3/8$ inch (9.5 mm) from one short edge, with equal margins extending past the top and bottom. Glue the $3/8$ inch (9.5 mm) turn-ins and fold them over the three edges of the paper with a small amount of adhesive, taking great care to avoid making spots. Next, pass a hot burnisher over it to iron the folded edge of the silk.

Then, cut out a strip of thin paper as long as the book's height and as wide as the shoulder. Use a small amount of adhesive to attach it to the backside of the silk, just below the covered template. When it is dry, carefully turn in the silk over the two ends of the joint strip.

For finishing the corners of the covered template, lift up the silk at the corner that has been glued down, and use scissors to cut them at a 45° angle. Glue them back down, making sure that the angles of the turn-ins meet cleanly. Use adhesive to attach the board sheet (template) to the board along with the joint strip at the shoulder, before pressing to close it.

▲Mounted silk end sheets

Next, prepare the part of the end sheet that corresponds to the book cover, that is, the fly-leaf. You're using silk without paper attached at this point. Carefully apply hot glue to the inside margin of the first blank leaf, and fold the silk over the edges to adhere it, using your fingers to smooth it down. Apply adhesive to the inside joint area of the second blank leaf, and press the first to the second. Leave the remainder free of glue.

When everything is in place, apply glue about $3/16$ inch (5 mm) from the edges of the second blank leaf, and glue it to the first one with a light squeeze in the press. Thus, no turned-in silk is visible.

Depending on your materials, you might be able to see through the silk to the paper beneath. To avoid this, you can put in a piece of colored or decorated paper on the inside when you prepare the end sheets. While it hides any possible defects, it also beautifies the whole binding.

▶ **3.** Folding the turn-ins to the inside

▼ **4.** A close-up showing how the corners are cut

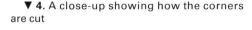

▲ **1.** Once the paper for the joint is in place, attach the template to the silk.

▲ **2.** Applying the adhesive for attaching the silk turn-ins

▼ **5.** The final attachment of the silk end sheets

Two-piece End Sheets

For this kind of end sheet, prepare the cover boards as you did for the two-piece ones in suede. Follow the same steps up to the point of covering with the leather. Before doing that, cut out and smooth the depression on the inside boards. When the leather on the outside is turned toward the inside, it must go into the depression that you made when you cut out the lightweight board. There is no way to fix this later if it doesn't happen.

Once you cover the book and make the turn-ins as described above, put in the leather joint (as previously explained); the joint also has to go into the depression. Once you attach the appropriate linings, cut out the template for the doublure from fine lightweight board. Cut it the same size as the depression inside the cover, minus the space that the silk will take up as it folds over (about $1/64$ inch [.5 mm] per side).

When you cover the template with the silk, glue it only on the back. It must form a rectangle whose obverse is free-floating rather than glued down. The doublure is now fitted and attached into the depression, since it is flush with the leather turn-ins.

When attaching the flyleaf, cut the silk to the size of the end papers, plus about $9/16$ inch (1.4 cm) per side. Cut a strip of paper as long as the book is high by about $3/8$ inch (9.5 mm). Use adhesive to attach the paper strip to the edge of the silk's backside corresponding to the shoulder. Fold this over and crease carefully.

Apply glue to the folded silk edge, and attach it to the first blank leaf so it touches the edge of the shoulder, overlapping the joint. When it's dry, turn in the excess margins of silk toward the inside of the first blank leaf, and then follow the same steps that were used for the one-piece end sheet.

▲ End sheets of suede and silk

▼ Silk moiré with paper backing made for binding

◄ 1. The guidelines and first cut for making the depression inside the cover board

◄ 2. Diagonal cuts made for removing the extra board

◄ 3. Leather turn-ins in preparation for fitting the silk doublure into the depression

►4. Template for doublure covered in silk and ready to be fitted and attached

PROCEDURES for LACED-IN BOARDS BINDING

- Disbind the book.
- Clean up and repair the signatures.
- Cut and attach blank end pages.
- Cut and attach waste sheets.
- Saw in the spine sewing stations.
- Sew the book and the end pages.
- Square the spine.
- Fray the cords.
- Glue up the spine.
- Trim the fore edge.
- Round the spine and trim the head and tail.
- Back the book.
- Cut out the boards for the covers.
- Bevel and sand the boards, except at the edge of the spine.
- Use paste to attach the frayed cords to the boards, protecting them with paper.
- Press the book for 24 hours.
- Remove and sand the excess paper, and fit the shoulders of the book to the boards.
- Apply glue for adding endbands and mull.
- Apply glue for attaching a paper lining.
- Cut out the lightweight board as the spine piece.
- Sand the lightweight board, and round it in spine former.
- Remove the excess glue from the spine, and attach the lightweight board spine piece.
- Use sandpaper to smooth and even out attached lightweight board.
- Cut out the leather, pare it, and attach it.
- Do turn-ins and endcaps, then set everything aside for 24 hours in the press to dry.
- Remove the waste sheets and excess glue at the inside joints.
- Make the template for trimming end sheets.
- Attach the end sheets.
- Leave the book in the press with the lightweight board between end sheets for 24 hours.
- Trim the flyleaf to the book.

▶ **1.** Preparing the silk flyleaf

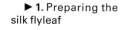

▼ **2.** Attaching the flyleaf to the leather joint

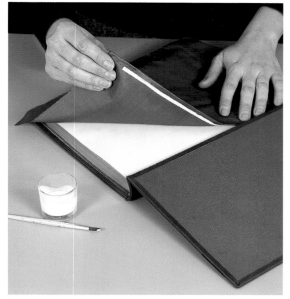

▼ Close-up of one-piece silk end sheet

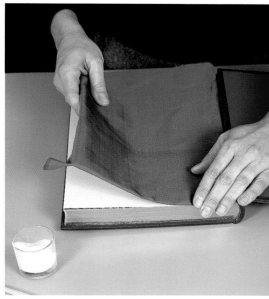

▲ **3.** Fitting the silk over the first blank leaf

▲ Completed silk and suede end sheet

Vellum Binding with Raised Bands

Because vellum is tough and inherently rigid, both the book to be bound and the vellum itself have to be handled with special care. First, prepare the book as with a leather binding. The cover boards for this type of binding are strengthened by the addition of two or three linings; or a heavier, thicker board is used along with one lining. When the time comes to bevel the boards, leave the edges proportional to the book's thickness.

Because vellum is somewhat transparent, the boards must be lined with white paper. Once the book has its boards attached and the lightweight board spine piece is attached to the spine, cut a piece of paper the same size as the book cover plus about $9/16$ inch (1.4 cm) per side. Coat it with glue and leave it flat on the workbench. Center one board of the book on one end of the paper with the three equal turn-ins. Turn the book over carefully so that the spine extends over the edge of the bench. Fit the spine to the paper, and then turn it over again and attach the remaining paper to the second board. Avoid wrinkling the paper, and, to ensure total adhesion, make certain that there are no air bubbles.

Once the paper is in place, do the turn-ins. In the process of doing this, you'll make some cuts at the spine and the corners. Turn in the boards separate from the spine. Trim the paper to about $3/16$ inch (.5 mm) from the spine's edge. This paper will be turned inside later when the vellum is attached.

Attaching and Lining the Raised Bands

Attach the false raised bands as usual, and sand their ends when they're dry, just as you do on a leather-bound book. However, due to the vellum's transparency, it's best to line the bands with white paper, just like the covers. Cut long strips of paper wide enough to cover the bands on the top plus the two sides. Apply a light coating of glue on one of

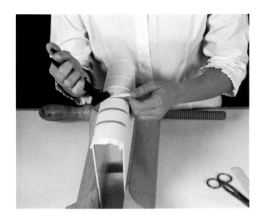

▲ 1. Lining the raised bands with paper strips

▲ 2. Molding the paper strips to the bands

▲ 3. When the vellum is moist, stretch it with your hands so it will accommodate the bands.

▶ 4. First phase of fitting the vellum on the spine

the strips, and attach its end on the start of the band. Use your thumbs to center the strip on the raised band.

When the band is totally covered, trim the strip of paper at the end of the band. Fit the remaining paper on the top over the sides, using band nippers or a bone folder to mold it down around the band. Trim off the excess with a knife. Now the book is ready for binding in vellum. It's not easy to find good vellum commercially, since it is used for all kinds of jobs from lamp shades to drumheads, and more.

Vellum

For bookbinding, use fine, thin vellum. This grade will adapt to the covers perfectly. In addition, it will be easier to mold down around the bands and the endcaps. As usual, you should cut it larger than the covers so it can be turned in around the boards.

The vellum shouldn't be thinned with a paring knife; rather, apply it just as it is. In preparation, moisten the spine area of the vellum with a ball of cotton dipped in water, and let it sit for a few minutes. Repeat this step several times until the material softens slightly.

When it's ready, gently stretch the vellum, without adhesive, over the spine to begin shaping the vellum over the raised bands. Once this is done, apply a coating of paste to the vellum. Then fold it in the middle just as you would the leather, and wait a bit until it softens. When you think it's ready, give it another coat of paste.

MAKING PASTE

To make paste, use three parts water to one of flour. By hand, break up any lumps that form. Place the pot over heat, and stir it continuously with a wooden spatula or an artist's brush. When the mixture begins to boil, remove it and set it aside to cool. Now the paste is ready to use.

Keep in mind that it's best to prepare the paste every time you need it, since it goes bad very quickly (it loses its adhesive effect after 24 hours). If you want it to last longer, add a few drops of formaldehyde.

► Wheat flour and water in a proportion of 1 to 3 for making paste

▲ The paste should be thick but free of lumps

MIXING METHYLCELLULOSE AND POLYVINYL ACETATE (PVA) ADHESIVE

This is a very clean type of glue that's easy to use because of its texture and ingredients. To prepare the methylcellulose, dissolve it in water to create a fairly thick paste. Next, mix it with PVA in a proportion of approximately 2 to 1.

When that's ready, fine-tune its thickness by adding a little water, keeping in mind that this kind of glue should fall in droplets from the brush, not in a stream.

► Materials ready for mixing methylcellulose and PVA

▲ Once the methylcellulose is dissolved, allow it to sit for a while. Then add the PVA and water to it to form the right consistency.

Binding the Book in Vellum

Binding the book in vellum uses the same steps as binding one in leather. With the palm of your hand, gently stretch and pull the vellum over the spine so the bands are visible. Avoid stretching it more than necessary. The more the vellum stretches, the more it will shrink when it dries.

When the vellum has conformed to the spine, attach it to the rest of the cover. Again, avoid stretching it too much. Once this is done, turn in the head and tail. It's possible that when you mark the back corners, the vellum will spring back to its original position. This means that it is still very elastic and needs more time to adhere to the shape.

While you're waiting, you can mark the raised bands again with the aid of the band nippers. To keep from scratching the vellum, drape a piece of cotton fabric on top of the bands. Don't rush the job of molding it down; rather, do it gradually, alternating it with making the endcaps and back corners.

When the endcap and back corners are formed as with leather binding, cut some pieces of lightweight board slightly wider than the book and insert them on the inside, between the covers and the end papers. Before inserting, make a fold lengthwise near the long edge, around $3/32$ inch (2.5 mm) that will fit between the shoulder and cover board. This will keep the vellum from pulling the board too tightly to the shoulder during the drying process and make it open poorly.

Fold the extra lightweight board at the fore edge back over the cover, protecting it from the subsequent tying up with cord that completes the molding of the bands. Tie the book with a strong hemp cord on each side of the bands to keep it secure as it dries and shrinks.

Let it dry for 24 hours or more. After this time, untie it and continue the process as if it were a leather-bound book with linings, end sheets, and so forth.

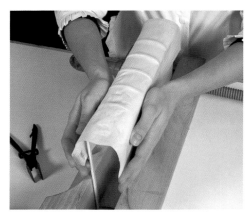

▲ **1.** Attach the vellum gently so that you don't stretch it too much.

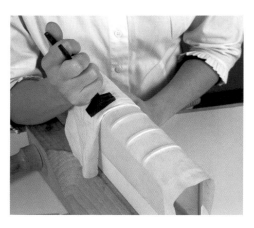

▲ **2.** Mold the raised bands with the protection of a cloth to avoid damaging the vellum.

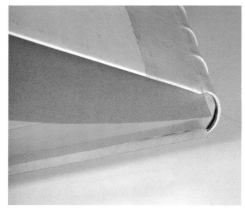

▲ **3.** Insert the lightweight board before drying.

◄ **4.** Tie the book up with cord to secure the molding of the raised bands.

► **5.** Book tied and waiting to dry

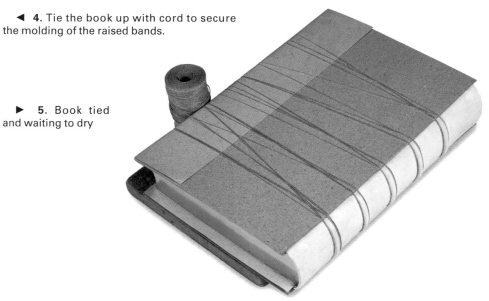

▲ **6.** Attaching the corners

► **7.** Close-up of finishing the corners

▲ **8.** Completed book in half vellum with corners

Binding in Vellum with Raised Bands

The method explained in this section was frequently used during the Renaissance and made it possible to use large, thick bands in spite of the vellum's inflexibility. This system can also be used in present-day bindings.

First of all, the raised bands (real or false) are lined separately with fine vellum, leaving a little extra material on each side of the band.

Then, trim the vellum to cover the entire book. As usual, leave adequate material for turn-ins. Next, use a pencil to mark the vellum where the bands are to appear on the spine, and draw their outline. Use a hobby knife to cut out this space to leave gaps for the bands to come through. After applying paste to the vellum, work as usual, making sure that the bands fit inside the gaps.

The finish on this type of book is commonly more rudimentary, but not necessarily lacking in beauty. You can create shapes on the spine that wouldn't be possible in any other way. These books are very elegant when calligraphy is used on the spines, and any possible lumps produced by the bands of vellum are disguised.

MODELING IN LEATHER

Within leather and vellum binding, there can be a variant, involving forming shapes in the leather on the boards of the book, as is done in the spine in forming the bands. This system is much more subtle and delicate and requires great skill to accomplish. It allows one to create various types of relief, geometrical shapes, and slightly stepped elevations toward the inside or the outside of the boards.

Shaping with Boards
This process involves placing boards on top of the book board to produce various elevations. When you use this system, you can never give the shape a 90° angle, because the book will become distorted when the leather is attached. Once the boards are attached, stretch the leather a little and allow it to soften. For that purpose, apply a thick layer of paste. When it has softened up, remove the excess paste, and apply another fine coat spread out thoroughly with a nearly dry brush.

When the leather is put on the book, it will also have to be moistened on the outside with a wet sponge. When the leather is wet, it's very sensitive to possible marks and scratches. You can even make the grain of the leather disappear if you apply too much pressure with your fingers, so always work with a cloth covering the table. To adapt it to the shaped boards, the book can be placed in the press protected by thick pads on each side that will help the leather adjust more effectively to the whole shape.

The finish must be done outside the press while the book is still moist. For this job, you'll use a bone folder or burin.

Attaching Shapes with Leather
Leather the same thickness as the cover leather can be used for inlaying shapes and designs. This is done by placing the new leather over the leather cover and cutting through both at a 90° angle. You can use the same leather as on the cover, or else leather in a contrasting color. The shapes can also be created with the covering leather. In this case, fold it and crease it before covering so that it forms different shapes and textures. This variant can produce very attractive results when the job is finished.

Antique Binding in Leather

Just as with binding in vellum, antique binding also involves a unique system for preserving written or printed documents. Knowledge of this sort of binding is not only useful for restoring books, but can be used in other situations.

Binding the Book in Leather

Sew the book just as you would antique vellum books. The cords of the sewing frame must produce raised bands on the spine, and once the book is sewn, these cords are cut to a length of $2^3/4$ to $3^1/8$ inches (7 to 8 cm) from the first and last signatures.

Use a needle to fray the cords so you can apply paste to them. Apply a thin layer of paste, and then roll them up with your fingers so they form a type of cone shape, from the base to their ends. They will be perfectly rigid when dry.

Next, trim and round the book, and then start to make the endbands at the head and tail. These can be made of linen thread, although they were commonly made of dyed thread. When you've trimmed the book and attached the endbands, apply a thin layer of hot glue to the spine so that the signatures and the decorative features at the head and tail are secured.

To complete this reinforcement, adhere small pieces of vellum between the raised bands to form a spine lining. Do the same for the top and bottom spine panels up to the endbands, to provide greater consistency. Sometimes, the cords from the sewing that make up the raised bands are also lined, in part to protect the sewing, and also, to smooth out any unevenness that may exist.

Attaching the Covers

This type of binding was made without backing. The cords serve to attach the cover boards, and since it was sewn with a stout linen thread, it swells naturally at the spine.

Until the 16th century, book covers were made of wood. Binders' board came into use in Italy later, and it soon spread throughout Europe. However, the construction of the cover is the same, whether from wood boards or binders' board. The binders' board must be quite thick and firm. It's cut out in such a way that there are ample squares along the three edges.

Use an awl to make two holes near the edge of the boards at the position of each cord, which is already prepared with paste and pointed at the tip. Insert this point from the outside to the inside of the board through the first hole, and bring it back out through the second hole. Repeat this step as many times as there are cords.

With the cords stretched, and the binders' board laced on, apply paste to the part of the board where the cords are attached. Once the paste is nearly dry, hold the book with your left hand at the fore edge. Place one of the covers on top of the table, and use a hammer in your right hand to pound the cords flat to reduce their thickness.

In the case of wood covers, make a small cut to accommodate the cords. Although they won't be totally hidden, at least they won't look too large when covered with the leather.

Leather for the Spine

The leather commonly used for the spine of this type of book is calfskin with no grain. It is pared down as usual on the sides, and a bit along the spine, which will have to be stretched somewhat to conform properly to the raised bands.

Next, apply paste to the leather to soften it. Place the leather carefully on the spine; you'll have to pull it to make it conform to the shape. Then, stretch it over the boards, and turn in the corners.

Since there's no lightweight board in the spine, the leather at the head and tail is turned in on itself. It's also good to avoid paring down the leather too much along the spine, especially at the head and the tail, since that would weaken it too much in this type of binding.

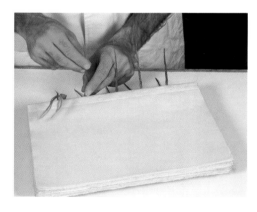

▲ **1.** Applying paste to the cord ends from the sewing

▲ **2.** Using an awl to pierce the cover boards

◄ **3.** Lacing on the board with cords stiffened by glue

▼ **4.** Boards laced onto the book

Attaching the End Sheets

When the leather is dry, add the linings and then attach the end sheets as if it were a clothbound book. You can also opt to use colored end sheets.

The book's finish is sturdy and unrefined, since the boards haven't been beveled and there is neither an endcap nor back corners.

The cords that attach the boards are visible on the front and back covers, but if they're done correctly, they provide a particularly beautiful finish. Even so, these slight protrusions will be disguised later on if the cover is tooled.

Paper restorers most frequently use this binding technique. When the reconstruction work is done, the book takes on an appearance that could be the same as when it was originally printed and bound.

▲ **5.** Use a bone folder to smooth out the pasted cords.

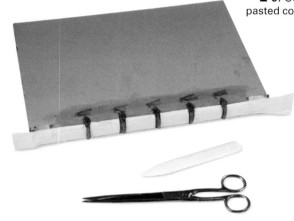

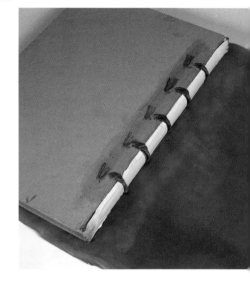

▲ **7.** The book with spine linings

▲ **6.** Hammer the inside of the cover, leveling the high spots.

▶ **8.** Close-up of the leather that has been trimmed and pared

▼ **9.** Attaching the leather to the spine

▶ **10.** Making the turn-ins

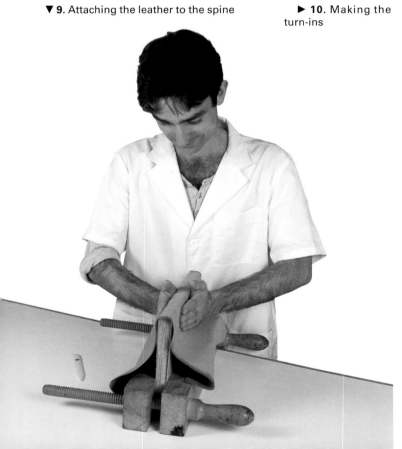

This chapter covers two important subjects: how to protect printed documents before they're bound, and how to protect bindings.

Light and oxygen discolor leather as time passes, and antique covers made of paper or lightweight board may weaken with the years. Nevertheless, the original covers shouldn't be replaced because they're a part of the book's history. Boxes and chemises serve to protect these books without compromising the value of the original pieces.

In addition to older examples, there are important literary works from the 20th century bound in publisher's cloth with a dust jacket. Many of these books have become collector's items over time, and need the protection of a box, which can be decorated as lavishly as you wish. The box adds value without interfering with the piece that's preserved inside.

Chemises
and Boxes

A wide range of portfolios, boxes, and chemises can be made for various purposes. Although we can't cover all the possibilities here, the following examples will give you methods and ideas that can be applied to any box or other protective covering.

Portfolios and Slipcases

These protective enclosures are commonly used for collectors' books waiting to be bound. Simple materials are used to make them, such as cloth and paper. The title of the work appears on the spine of the portfolio, either stamped directly on it or in the form of a leather binder's label.

The thickness of the board varies, depending on the size and weight of the material being protected. The best type of board to use is binder's board, which is very lightweight and practically immune to curling. In addition, it allows for a better finish with a minimum number of steps.

Making a Portfolio

For an unbound or sewn book, cut out two boards measuring $5/64$ inch (2 mm) more than the corresponding sides at the head, tail, and fore edge. The spine side, on the other hand, has to be flush. Once you've cut out the two panels, cut out the spine to the same height as the two boards and as wide as the thickness of the book plus the two boards.

Once the three pieces are cut to the desired dimensions, cut out the cloth or paper that will be used to cover the outside of the portfolio. Leave a joint space on both sides of the spine equal to two board thicknesses. Once you've covered the boards, line the interior with an appropriate material (perhaps the same one that's used on the outside or one that contrasts in texture or color). When the piece is done, allow it to dry under pressure.

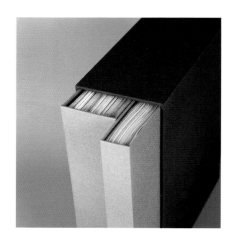

▲ Two portfolios inside a single slipcase

▲ Materials ready for making a portfolio and slipcase

▲ 1. First stage of making a portfolio

▲ 2. Lining for the portfolio's interior

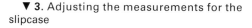

▼ 3. Adjusting the measurements for the slipcase

▼ 4. Assembling the slipcase after cutting out the board pieces

Making a Slipcase

Once the portfolio is dry, close it up and go over the spine side with the bone folder. Be sure to rub through paper so it doesn't create any shiny spots. Next, place the book inside it. Cut out the two panels and three edge pieces that will be used to make the slipcase. The inside of the slipcase can be lined before or after cutting the pieces, but it is best done beforehand.

Once you've lined the board on one side, cut out the three edge pieces. They should be as wide as the spine of the portfolio. Get this dimension by placing the book inside the portfolio, on top of the table. Then hold the lined board in a vertical position on the table, next to the spine. Mark the thickness of the portfolio with a pencil on the lined board, then cut out the three strips of board with the paper cutter. They'll be the right width; the length will be cut later.

Next, prepare the panels; they should be as long as the portfolio spine plus two board thicknesses, and as wide as the closed portfolio plus one board thickness.

Once the panels for the slipcase are cut out, adjust the length of the three edge pieces. Cut the edge piece that goes on the fore edge the same height as the panels, but cut the two edge pieces corresponding to the upper and lower parts the same width as the panels, minus one board thickness.

Assembling the Slipcase

Once you've cut out the five pieces and placed them on your workbench, you're ready to assemble the slipcase. Use thick PVA for that purpose, since it dries fairly quickly.

Place one panel of the slipcase in front of you, with the lined portion (which will be the inside) facing up. Next, use a small brush to apply glue along the long edge of the edge piece for the fore edge. In addition, apply adhesive to the one long and one short edge of the other two edge pieces. With glue applied to the three pieces, place the fore edge piece on one of the panel's edges, which will span the height. Apply some light pressure with your fingers to encourage adhesion. Fit the other two shorter pieces to the panel edges at right angles to it. Apply PVA to the three exposed edges of the edge pieces that are now attached to the first panel. Then place the second panel on these, and place a light weight on top while it dries.

While the glue is still moist, use a straightedge on the inside and the fingers of one hand to adjust all the parts so they fit perfectly. The edge pieces of the boards should form exact 90° angles.

▲ **5.** Placing the remaining panel of the slipcase on the edge pieces

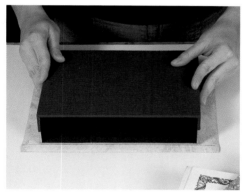

▲**6.** Adjusting the panels to the previously marked line

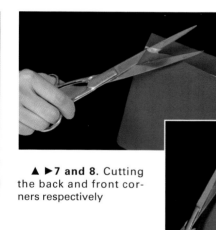

▲ ▶**7 and 8.** Cutting the back and front corners respectively

▲ **9.** Attaching the paper edge pieces

◀ **10.** Completed slipcases

Covering the Slipcase

Once the slipcase is dry and you've checked all the edges, finish smoothing it with sandpaper prior to covering it with paper or fabric. Cut two pieces of material the same height as the slipcase plus its thickness, and the width of it plus about $9/16$ inch (1.4 cm) for a turn-in, plus half its thickness.

Paste up one piece of material with adhesive and attach it to the slipcase. Take pains to leave about $5/8$ inch (1.6 cm) of material at the open edge of the slipcase so that it can be turned in. Once it's in place, turn in the material at the head and tail, using the palms of your hands. Glue it down carefully on the edge pieces of the slipcase, except for the opening and the fore edge, which you'll turn in later.

Use scissors to make a longitudinal cut in the front part, following the fold in the cloth. Once the appropriate cuts are made, all you have to do is turn in the material into the opening of the slipcase. However, to keep the material from bunching up too much, take the precaution of cutting the remaining cloth at an angle, extending over the head and tail edge pieces. Turn in these pieces next. Trim the corners of the material that correspond to the fore edge before turning in the material there. Cover the other panel in the same way.

Next, all you need to do is to cover the edge pieces after making certain the panel material doesn't overlap on them. If it does, double cut it with the aid of a hobby knife to eliminate any overlaps that might detract from the final appearance of the slipcase.

Cutting and Attaching the Edge Material

Now you're almost done with the slipcase because you're ready to attach the edge material, which will cover the edges of the material used on the panels. For that purpose, use the same material or a different one that contrasts with the first. Thus, if you're making a portfolio out of marbled paper, and you opt to protect it with a fabric-covered slipcase, you can attach the same marbled paper on the edge pieces of the slipcase. Various combinations help lend personality to the book that will go inside.

The material for the edges should be as wide as the opening of the slipcase. Both the upper and the lower edge pieces must be long enough to turn into the inside, and they must also overlap onto the fore edge. The remaining fore edge piece must be the same height as the slipcase. After you've cut out the edge pieces, attach all but the fore edge piece; it will be attached last, overlapping the other two to give the final finish.

Once everything is completed and dry, place the portfolio and book inside the slipcase.

▲ **1.** Use a chisel to make the cut when installing the ribbon.

▶ **2.** Once the ribbon is in place, glue it on the backside.

▼ **3.** The ribbon on the slipcase makes removing the portfolios easy.

▼Making a rounded spine (see page 91). The shaped spine can also be made with binders' board.

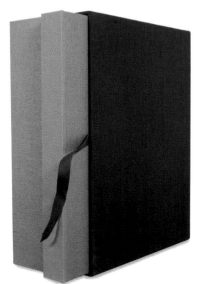

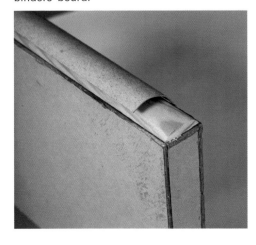

Portfolio and Slipcase with Rounded Spine

Making this kind of portfolio and slipcase involves the same steps we've already described in detail, right up to attaching the covering. Once you've assembled the slipcase, cut a piece of wood out in a half-round shape the same length as the slipcase. It's nearly impossible to make this piece the exact width you need. Fortunately, it doesn't matter if it's somewhat narrower than the thickness of the slipcase. Adhere it to the fore edge (now the "spine"), flush with the head and tail, and properly centered with respect to the edges.

Once it is completely glued on and dry, cut a piece of lightweight board the same height as the slipcase and as wide as the span from edge to edge of the slipcase going around the wood piece. Round it in the spine former. To attach it, we recommend using hot glue. Apply it to the portion of the lightweight board that fits against the wood. Due to the quick drying, quickly attach the rounded lightweight board and fit it carefully to both the wood and the slipcase edges so it adheres well.

Now you have a rounded spine, but it's not thick enough for stamping a title on the surface. If you wish to do that, you'll have to reinforce it with another piece of lightweight board that's cut and rounded in the same way as before. When this second piece is ready, apply glue to the spine, place the second piece of board on it, and rub it down. Once it's dry, use a hobby knife to smooth the edges to remove any excess glue and any extra board forming a ridge. Next, sand it with a sanding block.

Now, the round-backed slipcase is ready for covering, which can be of either leather or cloth, either quarter or full. The pasted up leather or cloth is pulled over the spine and onto the panels, with turn-ins (pared, if leather) extending over the head and tail edge pieces. After the material is in place on the spine, make some parallel, lengthwise cuts on the extra material at the head and tail to within about $1/32$ to $5/64$ inch (.8 to 2 mm) of the board's edge so the resulting strips overlap one another when folded inward. Next, flatten them with a few light taps of the bone folder. These turn-ins are covered with head and tail edge pieces that you cut (and pare, if leather) for this purpose and are attached practically flush with the edges.

▲ **1.** Attaching quarter cloth to the boards and spine of the portfolio

▲ **2.** Attaching the paper sides

THE INNER RIBBON

With this type of item, it's common to install a ribbon on the inside to aid in removing the portfolio and book without taking the slipcase from its shelf. The ribbon has to be installed right after cutting out the boards for the slipcase and before assembling them. Use a chisel or a hobby knife to assist in attaching the ribbon. Make an incision in the center of one of the panels for the slipcase, and pass the ribbon from the inside toward the outside. Allow about 3/8 inch (9.5 mm) to extend on the outside of the panel, and glue it down. When it's dry, strike it with a hammer to force it into the board and avoid creating lumps on the outside after covering. When that's done, continue as before.

▼ Portfolio with flaps for protecting the document and a slipcase with a rounded spine

▶ A series of leather-edged slipcases with their respective books

A Slipcase Edged in Leather

In contrast to the preceding slipcase, this one is used only for books that are already bound, whether to protect them or individualize them. The steps to make it are similar to the one already described, with additional ones that lend it a different quality with respect to the finish.

Preparing the Slipcase

The slipcase consists of two panels and three edge pieces. To begin, cut out two pieces of board about 1 inch (2.5 cm) larger than the covers of the book; then cut out one more piece, out of which the three edge pieces can be cut with room to spare.

Draw a pencil line on the panel boards, $9/32$ to $5/16$ inch (7 to 8 mm) from the edge where the spine of the book will be. At this point, glue on a piece of lightweight board the same size as the boards to produce a small step at the edge.

Use paper or velvety cloth to cover all of the slipcase panels, on top of the lightweight board, including the step and board that will make up the edge pieces. Finally, weight down the pieces, and allow them to dry.

Cutting Out the Boards

Once dry, cut out three edge pieces, making them as wide as the book is thick. (You'll adjust their length later.) Cut the panels the same height as the book plus the thickness of the head and tail edge pieces. To calculate the width, measure the book's cover, from shoulder to fore edge, plus the thickness of one edge piece. (The step produced by the lightweight board must remain intact, so don't trim it off.)

You now have two panels cut to dimension, plus three edge pieces whose length is yet to be determined. One of these edge pieces should be exactly as high as the panels. To cut the head and tail edge pieces, trim them to the full width of the book. Now you need to shape one end. Use a pencil to trace the spine's curvature on one end of each edge piece. Now, all you need to do is use scissors and a sanding block to adjust the curvature.

Preparing the Leather and Assembling the Slipcase

Once the five pieces are cut out, you'll prepare them for attaching the leather at the opening of the slipcase.

First, bevel the boards for the panels with sandpaper on the other side of the stepped edge to produce a 45° bevel that you can round off to produce a slight curvature. When everything is ready, cut out two strips of leather about 1 inch (2.5 cm) wide, somewhat longer than the panels for the slipcase. At the same time, cut out the leather pieces that will cover the curved part of the edge pieces at both the head and the tail. Cut them from a section of the leather that stretches easily, such as the animal's legs or belly. The pieces of leather must be thinned down as much as possible. Next, apply a coat of paste before attaching them.

Attach the leather strips for the two panels in the space that forms the step. Trim off the leather at the inside only. Once the leather is trimmed, fold it back and attach it over the beveled side.

Next, move on to the leather for the upper and lower edge pieces of the slipcase. Center it over the curved ends, about $1/4$ to $9/32$ inch (6 to 7 mm) on the inside lined surface, for subsequent turning in onto the outside surface. Pleat it with your bone folder, and trim it parallel to the curve.

Once the leather is dry, it can be burnished or left as is. Assemble the slipcase as described previously on page 89.

▲ Prepared materials for making a slipcase

▲ **1.** Placing the lightweight board along the drawn pencil line

◀ **2.** Lining the interior panels

▲ **3.** Lined boards cut to size and beveled

Finishing the Slipcase

Paste and smooth down the remaining extensions of the leather strips onto the top and bottom edges, then sand the three panel edges to 45°, excluding the leather edge. Use the sandpaper to give them a slight curvature.

With a hobby knife or scalpel and a straightedge, cut the leather on the panel near the opening about $^3/_{16}$ inch (9.5 mm) from the edge. Prepare some strips of cloth about 1 $^3/_{16}$ inch (3 cm) wider than the thick-

▼ **4.** Fitting the leather to the step at the inside front edge of the panel

ness of the slipcase, and glue them to the edge pieces to reinforce them. This will leave about $^9/_{16}$ inch (1.4 cm) extending over each panel so you can turn them in onto the panels. Check to make sure that no piece of cloth overlaps another (and if it does, trim it with a hobby knife). Next, trim out the cloth turn-ins to about $^3/_8$ inch (9.5 mm) from the edges of the slipcase.

Note that there is now a rectangular space on the panels made up by the leather on one side and the cloth on the other three. You must fill in this space with a piece of lightweight board or paper to even out the thicknesses. Once this is done, you merely have to attach the paper or cloth that will cover the outside. Do this as described before, while taking care to attach the material at the point of the curvature occurring with the leather on the board near the opening. In no case should this material turn in toward the inside of the slipcase.

Apply the edge pieces the same way, with the ends cut in the same shape as the head and tail, and glued in place very close to the edge. Follow this with the usual steps.

The Final Result

To lend the slipcase a slightly rounded shape, place a few pieces of cloth inside so it bulges slightly while it is still moist. You'll notice that the opening warps open somewhat due to the pressure inside. To counter this, wrap the slipcase firmly with elastic from a pharmacy or cloth tape. Then, let it dry. Next, unwrap it, take out the cloth, and place the book inside the slipcase. Leave a weight on it for 24 hours.

After this, the slipcase is finished and has a slight curvature from the center of the panel to the edges. You'll have a slipcase that's light in appearance and far removed from the stiffness that often characterizes this type of piece.

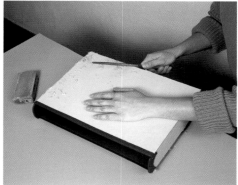

▲ **5.** Beveling the edges of the slipcase

▲ **6.** Trimming the edges of the leather

▲ **7.** Attaching paper on the panels

▼ **8.** Attaching paper to the edge pieces

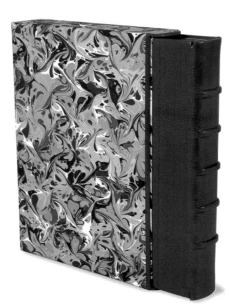

◀ **9.** Completed slipcase with book inside

One-piece Drop-spine Box

▲ A rare folio inside a drop-spine box

This type of box is made of two simple trays, one smaller and one larger, each with three sides. They close when one is inserted into the other.

To make this type of box, begin by making the base of the first tray, which is the smaller one. First, cut out the three edge pieces, as wide as the book is thick (the length will be adjusted later). The edge pieces help you to calculate the dimensions of the base. Make the base as high as the book plus the thickness of two edge pieces, and as wide as the book, including the spine, plus the thickness of one edge piece.

Once the base is cut out, trim the edge pieces to size. One should be as long as the base (the height of the book), and the other two as wide as the base minus the thickness of one board.

Once they're cut out, fit them together and attach them with PVA along three edges of the base and where their ends touch. After the tray is assembled, let it dry a moment before checking to see if the book fits properly inside it. Keep in mind that it is not yet lined, so the book should not fit too tightly.

To make the second tray, follow the same steps using the first tray you've made as a guide for measurements. Once you've finished, check to see that one fits properly inside the other, just as we did with the book.

Now you've produced two unlined trays with three edge pieces each, and one tray fits inside the other. Now, cut the board to make up the spine that holds together the two trays. Make it the same height and thickness as the second tray.

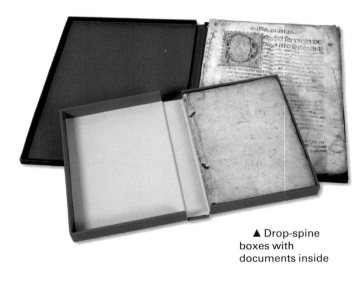

▲ Drop-spine boxes with documents inside

◄ **1.** Process of assembling a one-piece drop-spine box

▼ Drop-spine boxes personalized with the initials of the owner or library

▼ **2.** Covering fabric ready to be attached

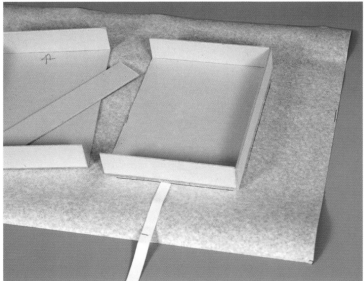

Cutting the Covering Material

Regardless of its size, a drop-spine box can be covered with a single piece of cloth, paper, or other material. To begin, place the three pieces you've created—the large tray, spine, and small tray—beside each other in order as if you're ready to attach the material. Leave two board thicknesses between them to form the joint spaces.

Place the open drop-spine box on top of your material. Use a strip of paper to measure the edge piece (wall) for the large tray from the outside edge of the box (where the side meets the table) over the wall and into the inside of the box, plus about 1/2 inch (1.3 cm) for overlap onto the base. Draw the outline of the spine and trays, and then draw a trim line outside of this rectangle using the added dimension taken with the paper strip.

Attaching the Material

Use thin PVA to paste up the material, and place the large tray in the position of its outline. Then position the spine and small tray on the material.

When the pieces are in place, move them to a cutting mat. Cut the material with a hobby knife so it fits the box, as shown in the photograph below. Make the cuts as follows: First, mark a triangle from the end of each box above and below the spine, then make a cut that goes from the upper vertex of the triangle, perpendicular to the edge of the material. Next, make a cut from the four outer corners of the trays toward the four corners of the material. Make a second cut from the four tray corners, nearly perpendicular to the edge of the material, and following the line indicated by the tray's head and tail. So that it can be inserted into the tray later,

make sure that the ends of the flap of the material created by the second cut is a bit narrower than the tray's inside joint.

Once everything is cut, fold the material toward the inside of the drop-spine box. First, turn in the small triangles at the head and tail of the spine. Next, glue the top and bottom flaps to the outer walls of the trays; there will be extra material extending past the tray edges toward the spine at the head and tail and past the fore edge of the trays.

Now, fold the material extending past the fore edge onto the outside wall, producing a 90˚ angle. Beginning at the inside tray corner, carefully cut the material at the fold along this angle (see photo 4). Glue down the resulting smaller flap inside the tray, covering the inside tray corner. At the spine, make a vertical cut on the head and tail flaps to the exposed corner of the head and tail edge pieces, and another one from that corner to the outside at about 90˚, forming a triangular-shaped side flap. Before gluing down the small side flap, use a bone folder to cover the exposed corner, much like you would the corner of a cloth cover.

Next, glue down the flaps at the head and tail into the trays, covering the inner walls and finishing on the base. Follow with the fore edge flap to complete this step.

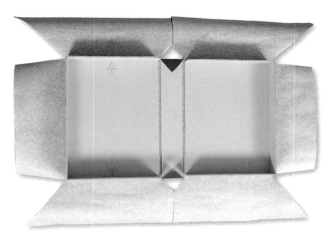

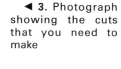

◄ **3.** Photograph showing the cuts that you need to make

▼ **5.** Close-up of the flaps covering the inside tray corner and exposed tray corner

▼ **4.** Cutting the angle at the inside tray corner

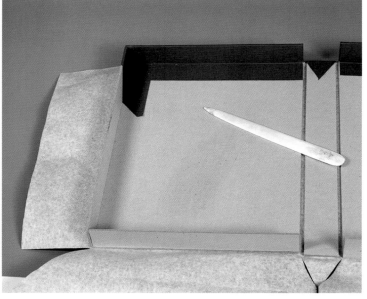

Attaching the Inside Lining

Once you've covered the drop-spine box, make sure it fits when it closes before continuing your work. Attach a liner made of thick paper or lightweight board inside the trays. In addition to making it stronger, the liner will help keep the tray base flat. It can also be used to even out any lumps produced by the material glued down on the tray base.

To line the inside of the box, cut a piece of material the same height as the large tray and as wide as the inside of the open box. Once cut, you'll install it in the smaller tray. Use a hobby knife to trim off the extra material so it fits in this tray with a "step" at the top and bottom edges.

Now you have a lining consisting of one wider part for lining the large tray and the spine, and a narrower part for covering the smaller tray's interior. Once you apply the adhesive to attach the lining, distribute it evenly. Use a bone folder to assure adhesion, with the exception of the joint spaces between the trays and the spine. Fit those with your fingertips so you can open and close the book.

After it's dry, place the book or document inside the box. Similar to book covers, the title can go on either the outside of the spine or the tray base.

▲ **1.** Lining the tray inside

▼ **2.** Installing the final lining in the drop-spine box

APPLYING THE ADHESIVE

If the adhesive dries out or loses its adhesion during the lining process, use a brush to apply more, and then continue your work. With large boxes, you can glue the base piece to the covering material first, attach the edge pieces, make the cuts, and paste up the flaps one at a time as you glue them down.

▶ Drop-spine box in full leather with onlays (by Josep Cambras)

▼ Completed drop-spine boxes

▼ Restored document protected inside its drop-spine box

This type of box is similar to the previous one, but, even though it appears to be made up of a single piece, it is made up of three pieces. It allows you to make a cover similar to that of a book with materials such as paper, parchment, or leather.

As described on page 94, assemble a tray with three edge pieces (based on the book's thickness) with a base of the book's height plus two boards and the book's width plus one board. Next, make a second larger tray based on the first one. Follow the same steps, making the base height that of the smaller tray plus two extra thicknesses of board, and the width plus one extra board thickness. This tray will have the same thickness as the first tray, including the thickness of the base board.

Now, the two prepared trays fit inside one another. Next, you'll cover them.

Covering the Trays

Cut two strips of fabric or other material twice the width of the large tray, plus an extra $3/4$ inch (2 cm). This distance determines the width of the fabric strips; you'll adjust their length later. Begin by gluing up and attaching the material onto the edge pieces of the large tray. Wrap the strip around the tray with the tray wall edges lined up with the center of the strip. Now you can cut the length of the material, allowing about $1/2$ inch (1.3 cm) turn-in extending past the head and tail edge pieces.

Once you've attached the material, you can cut the excess material at the tray base corners to assist in making the turn-ins that go under the base. Cut this angle with scissors beginning at the vertex formed by the board, then fold the material over the base. Now you can cut the flaps. Follow the line formed by the head and tail edge piece inner tray wall to make your cuts for the fore edge flaps so that they can be easily glued down to the inside of the tray.

All that remains to be cut are the ends extending past the head and tail edge pieces, where you'll make three cuts. Make the first cut perpendicular to the base at the joint formed by the head and tail edge pieces. Now you can fold the small piece of material as a turn-in onto the inside of the base. Make the remaining two cuts similar to that as in the previous exercise. Cut the head and tail flaps perpendicular to the exposed tray corners and about 90° from the corner toward

the ends. Use a bone folder to cover the corner, then turn in the end followed by head and tail flaps, cutting away excess material that might bunch up at the inside tray corners. Glue down the remaining fore edge flaps onto the inside tray walls and onto the base, rubbing the material down precisely into the joints. Cover the other tray in the same way.

You now have two covered box trays, and you need to address the interior. As in the previous exercise, you can attach a piece of lightweight board to serve as both a liner and fill-in to the material. Once the lightweight board has been attached, cut out the material to be used on the inside base; you can use the same material as you used to cover the tray, or another paper, felt, or other material. Cut it to the exact size, although you'll leave an extra $1/2$ inch (1.3 cm) on one side so it can be turned in under the base.

Making the Covers

Place the trays one inside the other in preparation for cutting out the cover boards. This cover will be like the ones for a book bound in cloth with a hard spine. Cut

▲ Boards cut for making the interior cavity of the box

▲ Drop-spine box with interior cavity, bound in full leather (by Josep Cambras)

the cover boards the same height as the trays, plus a $1/8$-inch (3 mm) square on top and bottom.

Cut their widths the same as the trays, plus a $1/8$-inch (3 mm) square, but this time on only one side. Once the boards are ready, cut out the spine piece. Make it the same height as the boards and as wide as the large tray thickness plus two board thicknesses.

You now have three pieces for making the cover, which you can put together once you've cut out the covering material. When you paste up the material to attach the boards, however, leave the thickness of one and one-half boards between the spine piece and the boards as a joint space. Cut the corners and do the turn-ins like a book cover. Then, line the spine's interior with any material you choose. This material should overlap about $1/2$ inch (1.3 cm) on the inside of the boards, to which you'll adhere one or two liners.

Once this is done, attach the trays onto the inside of the cover. Glue the base of the small tray, and adjust it until it is flush with the spine edge of the rear board; it must remain centered with respect to the head and tail. For it to stick securely, place it in the press, but not without first filling it with boards or cardboard large enough to protrude slightly to avoid damaging the edge pieces when pressed. Press the tray down onto the cover in the standing press with the covers open.

To attach the second larger tray, glue up its base and fit it over the first one, which is smaller and already glued to the cover. Close the cover onto the large tray, which is already glued up. Then, open up the box again, taking care that the tray doesn't come unglued. Put it back in the standing press, with the filler boards inside. Once it's dry, it's ready to hold the book or documents.

▲ You can place small books or tracts inside the box's cavity.

A Drop-spine Box with a Rounded Spine

▲ The inside of a box with interior cavity. Note the detail of the ribbon, which makes it easy to take out the book.

This type of drop-spine box has the same external appearance as a book. It can be covered in cloth or leather, depending on your preference. It is commonly used to hold important documents. As in the previous case, make two trays that fit inside each other.

Cutting out the Boards

Once the trays are covered, cut out the boards for the cover, which will be about 1/8 to 5/32 inch (3 to 4 mm) larger on the three sides than the large tray to form squares.

When everything is ready, cut a board for the spine piece the same height as the large tray and the same width as the large tray thickness plus the thickness of the two boards to be used in the covers. This spine piece serves as a base for making the core of the rounded spine, so bevel the side edges at a 45° angle.

After this is done, there are a couple of ways to create the desired curvature. For the first, you need a piece of wood in a half-moon shape that you can cover with a piece of lightweight board and fit to the previously beveled sides of the spine piece. In the second, you can replace the wood by board strips laminated together, rounded with a rasp and sandpaper, that can also be covered with lightweight board to fit to the beveled sides.

If you wish, glue one or two pieces of lightweight board on top of the false back to make it more rigid. When it's dry, sand the sides to eliminate any bulges. Then, line it with the material of your choice. Usually, a good fabric is used for this purpose.

Cut out the cloth, which will be as long as the spine plus 1/2 to 3/4 inch (1.3 to 1.9 cm) and not quite as wide as the spine's perimeter. Once the fabric is glued, place the flat part of the spine piece on it, centering it with respect to the four sides. Then, fold the material on the top and bottom sections, and glue it where the curvature is formed. Use scissors to cut off the excess fabric, making it flush to the curve. Glue the other two sides back onto the spine piece. Finish off both the top and bottom of the spine with appropriate endbands.

▲Cover with leather onlay decoration (by Josep Cambras)

Making the Covers

Next, you'll make the covers. You already have the boards for them, but still need to determine the spine. To do that, cut a piece of lightweight board to the same height as the covers and same width as the spine you've made. Take this measurement around the curved part.

Use sandpaper to smooth down the edges of this spine strip to a bevel, and make the covers with the material you've chosen: leather or parchment, for example. These are made in the usual way, depending on the material used. However, take care to leave a small space about 1/8 inch (3 mm) between the boards of the cover and the spine strip.

◄ 1. Pieces ready to assemble into a drop-spine box with a rounded spine

► 2. Molding the raised bands with cover flat

The Final Finish

After the covers are made and they're still moist, glue the rounded spine piece on the spine strip. Fit them together so that there are no bubbles, and allow them to dry. Then, open the cover and attach a strip of fabric on the spine; it should extend about $1/2$ to $3/4$ inch (1.3 to 1.9 cm) onto the cover boards. This fabric shouldn't be any longer than the spine piece and can be cut to a bevel shape on the boards so it doesn't stick out later under the trays.

Once done, install one or two liners. Then, as a final step, attach the trays at their respective places on the inside of the cover.

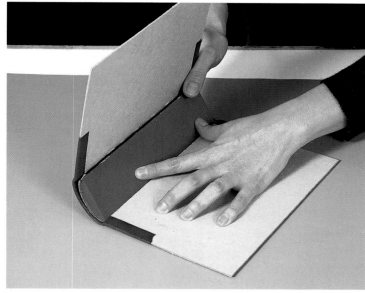

◀ **3.** Attaching the rounded spine to a cover

▼ **4.** The endcaps are worked as if you're dealing with a book.

▼ **5.** The finished interior part of the cover

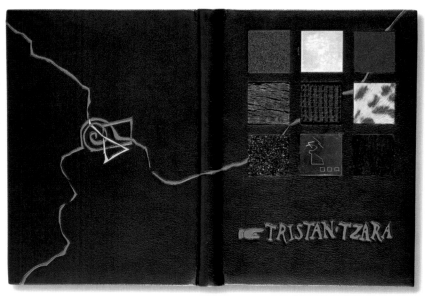

▶ Exterior of a full leather drop-spine box with rounded spine and inlays of various materials (by Josep Cambras)

A Chemise in Leather or Half Leather

A chemise is fitted to the outside of a book like a protective second skin. It is commonly used in a slipcase. It is sometimes made to reproduce the spine of the bound book, or it can add a decorative element to beautify the book. A chemise is almost always made to protect the binding from light, since light can alter the original colors of the leather.

Chemises range in their degree of difficulty to make. One of the most popular ones is the chemise that doesn't reproduce the raised bands of the binding but protects and fits the book by holding it at the fore edge.

Making a Chemise

Chemises are commonly made of board, but today there are new materials that not only simplify the task but improve the finished product. For instance, you can use fine offset printing plates. (It doesn't matter if they're used plates, because they'll be covered with paper and the surface will be covered.) You can cut them with a board shear or scissors as if they're binders' board.

First of all, you'll need two sheets of this material slightly larger than the book boards and four pieces of paper the same size. Apply a thin layer of contact cement to both the paper and metal plate. After a few seconds, glue the two together, and then put them in the press for a couple of minutes. Do the same for the back, repeating the operation with the two remaining pieces of paper.

Once the two sheets are prepared, cut them to the height of the book plus about $1/32$ inch (1 mm), and to the width of the book, plus about $3/8$ to $1/2$ inch (9.5 to 1.3 cm).

Now that you've made the panels, cut out the spine of the chemise from fine lightweight board. Make the spine the same height as the panels along the portion that touches the spine, and the same width as the spine of the book.

Attaching the Covering Material

The book's covering material can be in half leather, full leather, fabric, and so forth, depending on your taste. In this example, we've used leather to cover the entire chemise. First of all, thin the leather to about $1/64$ inch (.5 mm). Cut it a bit larger than the panels and spine so it can be turned in. Use

▼ Paper and offset plates for making the chemise panels

thin glue, and once it's applied, position the panels and the spine as usual, that is, with a joint space of about $1/8$ inch (3 mm) between them.

Turn in the leather of the chemise, and allow it to dry under weight, but not without first attaching liners to the inside of the panels. When it's dry, fit it to the spine of the book. Note that the fore edge of the chemise sticks out past the fore edge of the book. Use a pencil or awl to mark the fore edge of the book cover onto the inside of the chemise. This mark indicates the exact point at which the chemise must be folded.

Next, protect it with boards, and put it into the backing press. Only the fore edge that you need to fold in should stick out. Use a hammer to gently help with the folding, taking care not to damage the leather.

Once the two edges are formed at a right angle toward the book, line the inside of the chemise, whether in one piece or three (the spine and the two panels). Once the lining is in place, fit it to the book again, and use a bone folder to smooth the turned edges at a right angle toward the inside of the book so that the covers are supported at the fore edge. To remove the chemise, simply open the book.

▼ Close-up of folding over the fore edge of a chemise with a metal interior

▼ Attaching the plates and paper with contact cement

▲ The chemise must perfectly fit the book it protects.

A Chemise with Raised Bands

◄ Detail of the interior and exterior of a chemise with raised bands

To make this type of chemise, make an exact replica of the book out of binders' board. It must have the same dimensions, spine curvature, and bands as the original book.

After you do this, cut and thin the cover leather in the usual way. Once the leather is ready, moisten part of the spine area and fit it to the book's replica. Use the band nippers and bone folder so the leather conforms to the shape and size of the book, and holds this shape until it's dry.

Continue to make the chemise in the same way as the previous example, with the exception of using a removable template for maintaining a space for the spine (which will be lined on the inside with fine chamois leather). Thus, once the chamois is pasted to the leather, fit it onto the false spine and form it again with band nippers before allowing it to dry completely.

▲ Working the leather on a false spine for forming the raised bands

▲ Example of a binding, chemise, and slipcase (by Germana Cavalcanti)

◄ Two-volume work protected with both items inside a single slipcase

► A wonderful specimen of a binding, chemise, and slipcase (by Emilio Brugalla)

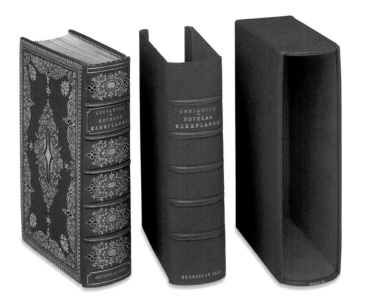

Decorating the *Outside Binding*

Once a book is properly bound, the title is added to it, and the book can be decorated. This decoration dignifies the book's contents as well as the owner, whether a private individual or a public institution.

Different books suggest different approaches, whether tied to the time during which the book was printed or its subject. In many historical cases, the outer decoration corresponded to contemporary artistic movements: baroque, neoclassical, romantic, and so forth. For instance, in the mid-19th century, the outside was decorated with images derived from the literature inside. As a result of the avant-garde art movements that took place in Europe beginning in the 1920s, as well as other influences, there are now an endless number of techniques and styles to illustrate book covers. The exploration of new materials plays an important role in this evolution.

Embossing with Foil and Composing the Title

Embossing is often used on simple books because it is quick and inexpensive. Gold is the most commonly used foil. However, other types are available in all colors with various degrees of heat and pressure sensitivity. Foils are available for different surfaces including fabrics, leathers, and synthetic materials.

These foils, whether gold, silver, or pigmented, are nothing more than polyester or cellophane film with the color on one side that is transferred with heat to the surface. Foils can be used with stamping dies or decorative rolls, and they're quite easy to use.

To transfer the design, simply place the pigmented part of the foil on the surface while applying pressure with a heated tool. The degree of heat you need depends on both the foil and the temperature of the material to be embossed. If you have no experience with this, experiment in advance to avoid making a mistake that could be difficult to fix.

To control the temperature of the tool, place a moist sponge inside a small container. Once the tool is hot, gently run it over the sponge. Depending on the noise the tool makes when it contacts the sponge, as well as how the water reacts on the metal, you'll have a fairly clear idea of the tool's temperature.

Foils transfer between 194 and 248° F (90-120° C). The tool's temperature can be estimated based on the boiling point of water or 212° F (100° C). In general, when the water merely evaporates on the metal, it hasn't reached the boiling point. When water reaches the boiling point it bubbles up on the metal, indicating that the tool is too hot.

Simply put, if water dropped onto the tool begins to boil, the tool is up to the boiling point. But if you do the same thing and the droplet is quickly repelled, it's because the tool is overheated and needs to be cooled with the sponge. Test the tool in this way to find the right temperature for foil tooling. At this point, you're ready to place the foil on the book.

▲ When a drop of water sizzles on the tool, it has reached the boiling point.

Embossing the Spine

To emboss the spine, you can use tools that stamp individual letters composing the title and author's name. You can also use pallets and decorative hand tools.

- **Pallets and lettering pallets**. Pallets used for embossing spines are illustrated as straight lines or various borders or patterns, and titling is done with lettering pallets that contain metal type. To use a pallet, mark the top of the lettering on the book's spine with the point of a pair of dividers, and place the foil on that mark. Make certain that it's lined up perpendicular to the spine's edge to guide the tool. (Naturally, this procedure must to be done with the book in the finishing press, and the tool's handle perpendicular to the book's spine.) With your left hand, hold the foil by the ends and keep it taut. With your right hand, rock the tool from right to left, pressing down evenly.

Do this decisively and energetically. If the tool (whether a pallet or a lettering pallet) is very wide, you must also move it up and down gently, almost hesitating, marking uniformly at both the top and bottom of the type or border. Use the foil's edge as a guide for moving the tool.

In review, keep these three factors in mind for the binding to be properly embossed: the tool's temperature, the pressure you apply, and the length of time that the tool contacts the foil.

▼ Various types and colors of foil for applying decoration and titles

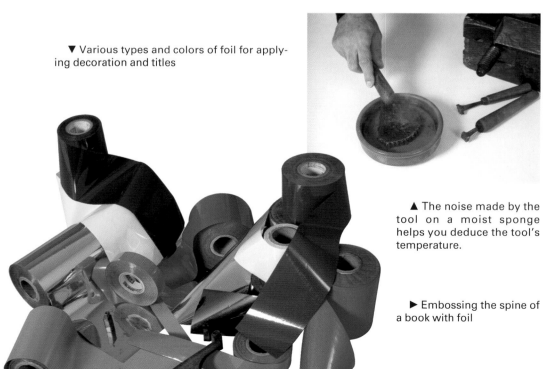

▲ The noise made by the tool on a moist sponge helps you deduce the tool's temperature.

▶ Embossing the spine of a book with foil

If the tool is too cool, it won't release the gold or pigment, and if it's too hot, it will burn the foil. Even though this seems obvious, keep this in mind for good results.

• **Decorative hand tools**. These are handled in a way similar to the pallets. However, start the process by using the unheated tool to make a light impression in the leathers, indicating the exact location for stamping, since foil covers the whole design.

To center a hand stamp on the spine, use the bone folder or a pair of dividers to trace a faint vertical line. This line helps you estimate where the sides of the tool should go in relationship to the spine's center. Once you've gently marked the hand tool on the spine, place the foil on it. For that purpose, find a point of reference for positioning the foil. This way, you'll be able to place the tool on the foil as accurately as possible to match the initial impression. This not only assures that the hand tool is accurate, but also saves gold in instances where the foil is made of that material.

Once you've impressed the decorative hand tool through the foil, use the bone folder to remove the vertical line that served as a guide. Pass it flat over the leather above and below the tooled impression without touching the impression at any point.

▲ Using foil to emboss the spine

▲ Locating the spine's center

▲ Connect two marked center points with a faint line as a guide for the stamping dies.

▲ Using the stamping dies with gold foil

Decorating the Sides

Pallets and decorative hand tools can also be used to decorate the sides, using the technique explained for decorating the spine. A roll, however, is the most important tool for this process.

There are two types of rolls: one for lines, or fillets, and one for borders or a continuous design. The former tend to be larger, and each one has a notch that's used to indicate the beginning and end of a line. The latter are nothing more than small cylinders or disks with a continuous engraved design. Common motifs are flowers, animals, and geometric figures. If the design connects at an angle, consider the motif you use, since some make the join more successfully than others.

To use a roll on leather, begin by marking a guideline on the sides with a bone folder. In the case of a fillet, it's preferable for the mark to have some depth so that the groove produced in the leather can serve as a guide for the fillet itself. When the roll has a design, make the mark as faint as possible so that it disappears from the pressure exerted when the decorative roll is used alongside it.

► Binding tooled with fillets and gouges

► An assortment of rolls

Once the sides are marked, place the edge of the foil strip next to the mark. Position the roll on top if it, and hold it with your right hand while you use your left hand to hold the foil loosely on the surface. Keeping it movable on the surface helps you to control where the roll goes and keeps the foil from crinkling.

If the roll is a fillet, roll it perpendicularly over the sides, moving forward continuously. If necessary, it's possible to go back over this line for corrections. If the roll is a decorative border, do the same thing, while also gently rocking it from the left to right to make the design clear in one pass, since it is difficult or impossible to go back over the design to make corrections.

▲ Continuous decorative roll and fillet

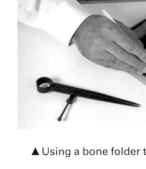

▲ Using a bone folder to mark a side

Lettering the Title

Brass type, mounted in a lettering pallet, is often used for book titles. It is similar to printing type but much harder and heat-resistant. In addition to the alphabet, spaces of various sizes are made to fit into the lettering pallet.

The title may occupy limited space on a book, whether because of the binder's title, the arrangement of the bands, or the spine's thickness. Choose the size of the type accordingly. Hold the lettering pallet in your left hand with the wing nut on the opposite side, slightly inclined in that direction.

To compose the title, place a space in the pallet and then position the type. If there's

▲ Beginning a fillet at a notch

▶ Holding the foil with your left hand to keep it from crinkling as you roll on top of it

more than one line, begin with the last one. After putting in a space, the next-to-the last line can be set based on the size of the type and spine.

Each piece of type has a mark known as a notch at the bottom indicating the position of the type in the lettering pallet. Even though it's easy to see if a letter such as a capital A is positioned correctly, this doesn't hold true for all of them. Type must be placed from right to left, notch up and facing you.

After the book title is inserted in the lettering pallet, tighten the wing nut with your right hand to secure the type. Heat the pallet and type, and secure the book in the finishing press, then emboss the book, keeping the wing nut on your left. The initial composition will be in the correct place when you turn the lettering pallet with the type facing down. Remember, begin with the last line and then continue in succession. This assures that the completed part is covered up with the foil and the remaining guide marks will remain visible.

◀ Clothbound books ready for lettering the title

▶ Several lines arranged in a lettering pallet

▲ An assembled title in the lettering pallet. You can see the notch on the lower part of the loose type.

▲ Mark the title with the aid of a pair of dividers.

COMPOSING THE TITLE

To emboss titles with foil, use the side edge of the foil as a guide. Making the title look elegant and balanced isn't easy. If you don't have much experience, follow these guidelines to achieve good results:

1. The bottom line of the title should be wider than the rest; if necessary, any articles and prepositions should be placed to the left of this line, although this will not always be feasible.

2. With only a few exceptions, articles and prepositions are never placed at the end of a line. Instead, center them between two lines or on the left side of a line.

3. The lettering of the author's name should never be larger than the lettering of the book's title. Nor should it be longer than the title's longest line.

4. The size of the letters within a single title can vary, depending on their importance in the context.

5. A small hyphen known as a dash rule is commonly inserted in the space between the author and the book title.

6. The distance from the base of the last lettered line to the fillet line that marks the title label should be the same as, or very similar to, the one between the top of the lettering of the author's name and the upper fillet line of the author label.

7. Independent of the title's length, the binder's label must be proportional to the book size and shape, with the lettering larger or smaller in accordance with the space allowed.

8. In cases where a single title is made up of several volumes of different sizes, there are several possibilities for stamping the text: Compose the title of the thinnest volume first, and use it as a guide for the remaining volumes. After composing the title on the thinnest volume, letter-space the title on the thicker ones using type of the same size.

If you have a large collection of volumes of different thicknesses, use the previous options, or use the same composition with different typestyles—part in one typeface and the other half in a condensed form of that face.

9. Sometimes, because of the work's importance, the date and place of publication are noted on the spine, along with the name of the printer. This information is commonly placed at the base of the spine, although it can also be placed between raised bands on a panel in smaller lettering, giving it the same emphasis as the author and title.

10. Even though the lettering on the spine serves to quickly identify a work, you must also remember it's part of the decoration and the book's aesthetics. In some cases, letters that are too large or small can clash with the look of the book.

▼ Stamping the title of the work on a leather binder's label

▼ Samples of various titles

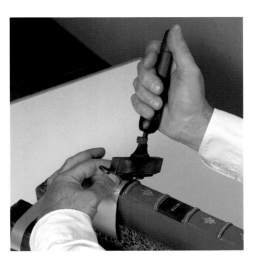

Blind Tooling

Blind tooling is a technique used for tooling the leather by means of heat and moisture that forms the basis for embossing with gold leaf. Blind tooling has been around longer than bookmaking and has been used to decorate books since their inception. It originated with the Muslims. It can be used with all types of tools for decorating books, including straight and curved stamping dies that can produce an endless number of designs and shapes on the leather.

How to Blind Stamp Designs

The decoration on the spine of a book can include one or more designs. In cases where there's a single design in each panel between the raised bands, establish a well-centered vertical line on the spine, and center the tool on it. Based on the size of the design, use a pair of dividers to measure the panel and mark the center on the vertical line.

Once you've done this, use a brush to apply water to these marks. After the leather absorbs the water, make an impression lightly with a slightly warm tool held vertically.

Once all the designs are tooled and any corrections are made, apply the water again with a brush, this time to the whole space covered by the tool. When the leather reabsorbs the water, center the hand stamp on the impression made earlier. Use light pressure, perpendicular to the spine, to impress the hand stamp. Slant it toward the left as you lift it off and then return it to the initial position. Repeat this step, but this time, slant it in the opposite direction, that is, to the right.

▼ Various stamping dies

▲ Blind tooled book (by Josep Cambras)

▲ Blind tooling lines at the base of the raised bands

At the end of this step, the tooled leather will be slightly tan and get darker as you repeat the exercise on the dampened leather. Keep the tool at a very low temperature so that you can almost touch it with your bare hand. In other words, if you pass a moist finger over the tool, the water sizzles slightly. All the designs should end up close to the same color and intensity, so use the first one as a guide for the remaining ones.

Through consecutive imprints, you'll be able to change the leather's color. Be cautious about the temperature of the hand stamp; if is too hot, it will burn the leather, and you won't be able to correct it.

To finish up, apply a swab dipped in a little oil to the tool's face, and then repeat this step for a distinct, shiny finish.

Blind Tooling with Rolls and Pallets

Once you've used the bone folder to mark the leather where you plan to use the roll, moisten it with a piece of cotton or a brush dipped in water. As we've already explained, keep the roll at a very low temperature. In contrast to the stamping dies, you can't go back over the impression a second time. That's why you must pay special attention to how moist the leather is and how hot the tool is.

Note that all rolls have a beginning to their design. It's a good idea to mark this clearly with a pencil or an awl on the side so that you don't have to lift up the roll as you work.

In general, when you tool with a roll on a side, it's because you want to apply an ornamental border, so take care with the corners so they're finished off properly without going over them a second time. For this reason, slant the tool a bit at the beginning; it must form a 45° angle, which will be matched by the border that meets it.

Just the same as tooling with foil, make a slight back-and-forth movement from right to left to produce a thorough impression. In the case of blind tooling, the roll also has to be moved forward and backward in small increments so the color on the leather darkens.

▼ Blind tooling curves on a book panel

▲ **1.** Using a pair of dividers to mark the blind line

▲ **2.** To mark the line along the spine, measure from the marked fore-edge line with a strip of paper.

The process of blind tooling with decorative pallets on the spine is very similar to the one used with rolls, and in this case, it's very difficult to go back over the designs.

Blind Tooling Lines

For this technique, a line pallet is more commonly used than a fillet because this tool is more precise. To begin, mark a line on the leather with the bone folder and a straightedge to mark where the tool will be used.

Once the line is marked, apply water to it with a brush. Always begin with the tool at a low temperature. Contrary to appearances, the line pallet is curved slightly between the ends. So, if you place it flat on the leather, neither the right or left end contacts the surface. This is important to notice when you're blind tooling a line. Once the leather is marked and moistened, use the line pallet at a low temperature with the beveled part facing away from you.

For a smooth, uninterrupted line, place the back end of the line pallet at the beginning of the marked line to avoid driving the front end into the leather. To continue, push the line pallet on the leather along the marked line, with or without a straightedge. Repeat this step two or three times until the line is straight and uniform in color. End the line cleanly by rocking toward the front end of the tool. Exert light but effective pressure without forcing it. To keep the leather from scorching so that the color darkens progressively, keep the line pallet's contact time to a minimum. Finish off the line by rubbing a cotton swab saturated with oil over the tool's face and going over the line again.

▲ **3.** Using the bone folder to mark the lines for a frame on the sides of a book

◄ **4.** Blind tooling a line with a line pallet

How to Blind Tool a Title

Blind tooling a title is very similar to blind tooling a design. Once the type is arranged in a lettering pallet and guidelines are created, impress the center of the pallet onto the book's spine. After moistening the leather, press again on the center, then tilt it left and lift it off. Repeat this step from the center and toward the right. Repeat as many times as necessary until the letters are clearly defined. (The line is marked in two steps because the moist leather can yield under the pressure of the hot tool if done in one step, and the title can shift and end up in a different position when the operation is repeated.)

▲ Mudejar book decorated with onlays using lines and gouges (by Josep Cambras)

Special Leathers for Blind Tooling

There are various kinds of leathers, and not all of them are suited for blind tooling. Blind tooling leathers need to be of a certain thickness and porosity. Fillers and coatings that are sometimes used by tanners to even out the color or cover possible imperfections are a major enemy of blind tooling. Even though it's difficult to detect a coating or filler, there's a simple, quick way to see if the leather's ready for blind tooling. Simply moisten a spot on the leather with a little water. If it soaks in quickly, you can be almost certain that the leather will provide a good finish for blind tooling.

There's also a possibility that the water won't soak in while you're in the middle of a project. In such cases, you can open the pores if you gently strike the leather with a brush containing flexible bristles. Because it's easy to handle and is the right size, a toothbrush works well for this purpose.

▲ Mudejar composition (by Josep Cambras)

▼ Binding in the style of Aldo Manuelo on yellow leather (by Josep Cambras)

▼ Gothic-Mudejar binding done with small tools (by Josep Cambras)

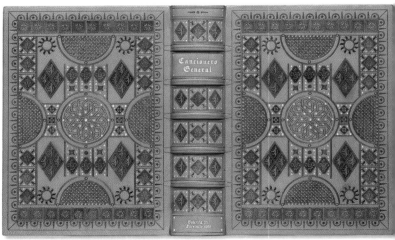

When you apply decoration to the sides and the book's spine, last-minute adjustments aren't beneficial. You should know in advance what type of design you're going to use and how to apply it.

For this reason, cut several pieces of paper the same size as the design you're going to create, whether for the sides, the spine, or the panels between the raised bands.

Use an ink pad, available at a stationery or art supply store, to coat the face of each tool. Then, reproduce the design on the paper to make the composition, much like putting a puzzle together. If your first attempts don't work, just keep trying out new ones until you're satisfied.

It's also a good idea to use a piece of thin graph paper with small squares to help center the stamping and line it all up on the sides without having to use a straightedge or a pair of dividers.

The Preliminary Drawing

Straight lines can simply be drawn on the paper with a pencil so you can reproduce them on the leather in the same size later with the fillet or line pallets. In contrast, gouges (curves) must be marked on the paper with ink, as you did with the stamping dies. For that purpose, use the inked impressions of all the gouges and line pallets on a piece of tracing or similar paper that shows what is beneath it. Pass this paper over your design to find the correct gouge or line to ink over your hand drawn design.

After the gouges and lines are marked in ink, number them on the paper to correspond with the numbered gouges and line pallets so that they can be easily accessed later on.

When the design is fitted to the paper and sized correctly, fit it to the side or spine of the book. Attach it at the edges with adhesive tape that won't damage the paper when it's removed.

Marking with the Tools

Once the design is attached, go over it with the appropriate tools that have been previously heated a bit with the finishing stove. Use gentle pressure until the marks appear on the leather through the paper pattern.

Lift the paper at one end to check the marks underneath. If part of the design isn't reproduced well, reposition the paper, still attached at one end, and go back over that section.

After the leather is marked and the paper removed, focus again on the book; that is, "caress" it with the slightly hot tool to define the design or touch it up if it's slightly out of alignment. Once the initial impressions are made, you can blind tool it using water and a brush as previously explained.

▲ Hand-tooled cover with design created using small tools (by Josep Cambras)

► Before applying the decoration to a book, do a preliminary drawing on paper.

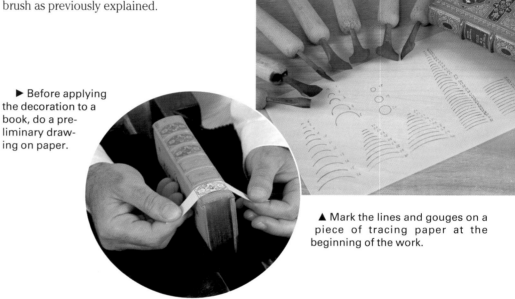

▲ Mark the lines and gouges on a piece of tracing paper at the beginning of the work.

▼ Different types of spine decorations on books and slipcases (by Josep Cambras)

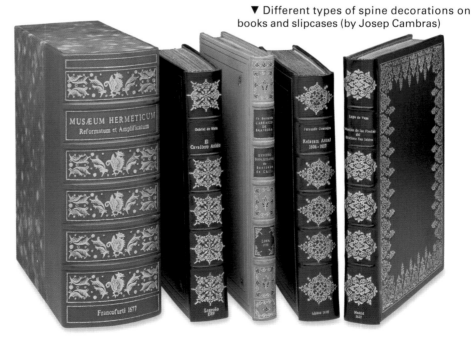

Gold Tooling with Gold Leaf

Gold leaf is the "royal treatment" for decorating books, but, because of its complexity, many bookbinders leave it off when they create their bindings. This technique requires lots of practice, both in stamping with foil and in blind tooling. It also requires a steady hand and great concentration. Using different pressure with the tools or going back over the designs can make the design inferior and not worth the time-consuming effort. The basis of good gold tooling is completely uniform blind tooling.

Materials and Tools

Once the book is blind tooled, rub it with a cotton swab dipped in paste diluted with water. Then use another piece of cotton dipped in vinegar to remove the paste. Use a third piece of dry cotton to dry it off. Remove any grease from your hands in preparation for gold tooling the leather.

- **Applying the gold**. Use a synthetic glaire or egg glaire to attach the gold. Synthetic glaire is a commercial preparation, and egg glaire should be prepared just before it's going to be used.

- **Preparing for gold tooling**. In choosing between synthetic glaire or egg glaire for gold tooling, it's best to use egg glaire for the rolls and synthetic glaire for everything else. Egg glaire can be used for only a few hours after applying it, whereas synthetic glaire allows much more time, thereby facilitating the bookbinder's work.

Once the book is blind tooled and clean, allow it to dry completely after the paste wash and vinegar are applied. Use a fine watercolor brush to apply the synthetic glaire or egg glaire to the blind impressions on the spine or book's sides. Do this carefully and neatly, since no part of the blind tooling should be left unglaired. Air bubbles on the blind tooling indicate areas with no liquid synthetic glaire.

While you wait for the book to dry, gather the rest of the tools and materials needed to complete the process. These include a gold cushion, booklets of gold, a knife to cut the gold, sweet almond oil, a cotton swab, some cotton, a cotton rag, and a small container of refined naptha (lighter fluid).

Apply a small amount of talcum powder to the cushion with the knife to remove any oils that might be on the surface.

Place two sheets of gold on top of one another on the surface. After administering a couple of light, angular blows with the knife to attach them, cut them to the desired dimensions.

Rub a cotton swab in a bit of sweet almond oil and apply it to the design or line that you want to gold tool. Hold the gold piece by its ends with your fingers, and place it carefully on the oil-coated leather. The oil you applied will make the leaf stick in the right places and making it easy for you to remove the excess later. Use a clean piece of cotton to impress the gold into the bottom of the tooled impressions.

Repeat this process as many times as necessary, based on the number of designs to be gilded. Although it's not necessary to fill up the book's entire surface, you should go ahead and apply gold to all areas that you wish to gold tool so you can take advantage of the tool while it's hot, and work quickly and securely.

Marking with the Tools

Once the gold is positioned, heat the tool in preparation for attaching the gold. Once the tool has reached the desired temperature, rub it on the back side of a piece of leather to clean off any impurities that might be present. Get your bearings both by sight (since the blind tooling is visible through the gold) and by touch. Don't grip the tool tightly as you go over your impression. Be patient, and once it fits into the impression, press down lightly but firmly. It is preferable to go over the same impression several times, keeping the pressure and sheen uniform. If you tool just once, you run the risk of scarring the book by tooling too deeply.

▲ ▶ Making a swab for the sweet almond oil

▲ 1. Items needed to prepare the egg glaire

▲ 2. Shaking up the vinegar and egg white mixture in a jar before setting it aside for a few minutes prior to using it.

◀ 3. After the contents of the jar have settled, tip it and pour out the clean egg glaire underneath the bubbles.

▶ 4. Applying the liquid egg glaire with a small brush

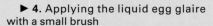
◀ Applying a double layer of fine gold

After you've used the tools, remove the extra gold with a cotton cloth. To do this, wind the cloth around your finger, and use it to gently wipe the section to be cleaned. The area around the designs that are gold tooled will be smeared with gold. Remove this residue with a cotton cloth moistened with a bit of naptha (lighter fluid).

When the surface is clean, apply a second single layer of gold leaf with no synthetic glaire. Once it's tooled and cleaned, go over the shape of the-stamping dies and lines again with the point of a

▶ Cutting the gold on the gold cushion

▲ Lacing gold on the inside turn-in of a book

moistened, flexible toothpick to avoid damaging the leather, allowing you to remove the extra gold from the design edges made with the tools. In case there is any error in the tooling, simply apply a little synthetic glaire with the brush to gold tool it again. For a good finish, you might need to apply two more single layers of gold.

In summary, the steps to carry out after the blind tooling are as follows: one double layer of gold, a single layer of gold, cleaning and correcting (if necessary), and two single layers of gold. At the very end, polish it to give it the final finish.

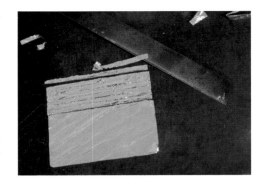

▲ Gold leaf cut into fine strips for gold tooling

▲ Various types of tools used in gold tooling

THE TEMPERATURE OF THE TOOLS

The egg glaire and synthetic glaire require different temperatures for gold tooling. If you take a drop of water and put it onto the hot tool, it must begin to boil in order to tool with the egg glaire. On the other hand, if you use synthetic glaire, the water should evaporate gradually. If it doesn't, the gold tooling won't work. Thus, if you're a neophyte in this field, it isn't inappropriate to do a few trial runs on a piece of leather in order to find the right temperature.

Gold Tooling with a Decorative Roll

When you use a roll, there's no way to blind tool it in advance. It has to be tooled based on the guideline at the edge, just as we did with the blind tooling. Use egg glaire for tooling it.

Once the leather is prepared, use a brush to apply a layer of egg glaire to the whole length and width of the area over which you intend to pass the roll. After it has dried for a few minutes, apply a second layer to the same area in the same manner.

When the egg glaire has dried again, proceed as you did with the stamping dies, applying the oil and gold leaf. Then, push the roll forward from the start with slight back and forth movements while rocking left and right all the way to the end. Don't go back over it or back up.

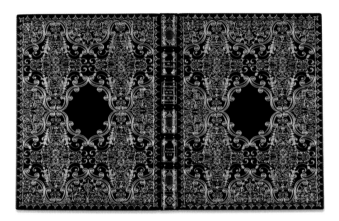

◄ Example of a baroque-style book with small onlay patterns (by Josep Cambras)

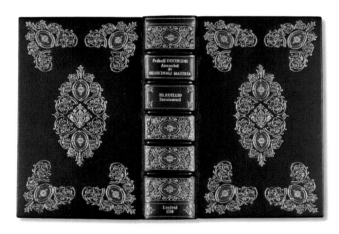

◄ Lavishly embellished spine (by Josep Cambras)

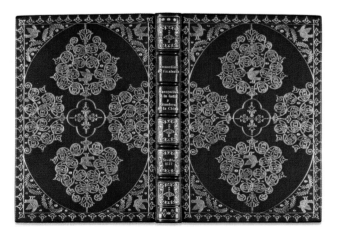

◄ Binding in Gascon style (by Josep Cambras)

Stamping with a hot stamping press is nothing more than a simplified form of manual gold tooling or embossing, but that doesn't mean it's any less beautiful once it's done.

This type of stamping reached its height in the 19th century, when book publishing became more prevalent. During this period of industrialization, workshops were able to increase their production of books.

The hot stamping press is made up of two adjacent metal platens that function by means of a lever on the right side operated by hand.

The metal die is attached to the upper die that is heated during use. The design is reproduced on the book's cover placed inside the press between guides in order to ensure proper positioning.

▲ Zinc die with corresponding template ready for installation in the press

Stamping Dies

These stamping dies, used for decorating books, are nothing more than $1/4$-inch thick (6 mm) metal dies made with a photoengraving process. They last for a long time and are used for long production runs as well as individual books. They can be used more than one time. Like other types of dies, the stamping dies have an engraved design that is faithfully reproduced on the book covers and can be gold stamped, blind stamped, or color stamped with foils.

Attaching the Dies to the Top Platen

In the past, the dies were attached to board with strong, fairly thick glue. This step was repeated to attach it to the appropriate place in the press, which was heated in advance. The extra board was then later removed by cutting. Now there are synthetic adhesive films for attaching the die directly to the machine.

In this case, the dies are placed facedown on a lightweight board, and this in turn is attached to a piece of heavier board. When everything is in place, the assemblage is put into the stamping press and squeezed tightly to assure that the relief of the stamping dies is reproduced and pressed into the lightweight board.

Using scissors or a hobby knife, cut out the reproduced designs. Attach the designs to a piece of board with the exact dimensions of the book cover. Once it's dry, position the stamping dies in the impression made in the

▲ Operator applying gold stamping techniques

lightweight board, and place a small piece of the synthetic adhesive film on the back of them.

When everything is ready, set the guides on the press in such a way that the dies are centered inside. With the machine heated, apply light pressure with the lever so that the dies attach to the upper platen and are ready for use in stamping the book cover that will be put into the press. Use the same guides to insert the book cover into the press.

The pressure, temperature, and time that the book and die contact one another are the same as that of stamping with foil. The techniques that were explained pertaining to blind tooling and gold leaf tooling are also the same.

◀ Different dies for stamping books

▶ Binding showing an embossed rectangular design on the front cover (by Josep Cambras)

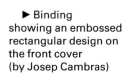

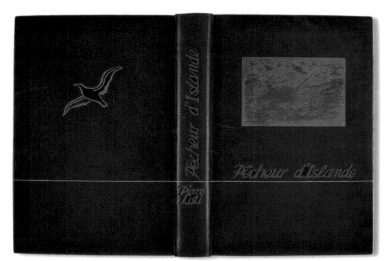

Gilding Edges and Gauffering

Gilding Edges

Gilding edges consists of applying gold leaf to the pages of the book where they're trimmed, whether only on the top edge or on all three sides. In addition to beautifying the whole book, gilding also provides better protection for the book, since it keeps dust from getting into the pages by closing up the spaces between them.

To gild the edges of a book, begin by cutting out some pieces of board the same length as the book. Place these flush with the edges inside the finishing press, squeezing as tightly as possible.

Once everything is in place, go over the surface with medium-grit sandpaper, followed by fine-grit sandpaper, and then with an even finer grade of sandpaper until the surface is completely smooth.

Use a small sponge to apply a layer of thinly diluted paste to the edge, and then use pieces of porous paper to rub it and remove the paste so that the edges shine.

When that's done, use a sponge to apply a layer of slightly diluted Armenian bole. While the bole dries, prepare the gold by cutting it on a cushion to the desired dimensions.

Apply a thick layer of egg glaire (that has been previously dissolved in about 3.2 ounces [96 mL] of water) to the edges. Place the cut gold along the edge, over the bole and egg glaire, beginning at one end and finishing at the opposite one. Then, let it dry.

There are several ways to know when it's dry enough. One is to check how dry the boards are. Another is to breathe on the gold and determine how long it takes for the moisture to evaporate (if it evaporates from the ends fairly quickly, it should be dry enough; if it is slow, you should wait longer). It's difficult to get it right on the first try, so it's a good idea to repeat the process several times.

When this step is done, apply wax to a piece of paper. Place the waxed side up the edge of the book. Burnish it with an agate burnisher in a direction perpendicular to the leaves of the book so that the gold is well attached and has a matte finish. To create a shiny surface, polish the edge with a fine cotton or silk cloth with wax on it to apply a layer over the gold, which will allow the burnishing tool to glide over it. Burnish the whole edge directly to produce the desired gloss.

If you plan to gild all three sides, begin with the fore edge that has already been rounded, then do the head and tail.

► Materials for gilding the edges

◄ 1. Using a sponge to spread the bole on the book's edge

▲ 3. Using an agate burnisher to set the gold on the surface with the help of waxed paper

▲ 2. Attaching the gold leaf. Note the position of the fingers, which keeps the gold in the right place.

►4. Final burnishing with the agate burnisher

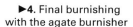

Gauffering

Gauffering the edges of a book is a further refinement of a book's gilding, but you should be accomplished in drawing to create a design. Once the edges are gilded, various decorations can be added to them using different techniques. All of these are based on the same principle: faithfully reproducing the desired design on a piece of paper with the same dimensions as the edge. When the drawing is ready, attach it to the boards that support the book so that it matches up perfectly with the gilded pages underneath it.

• **Geometric designs**. If the designs are geometrical, mark them through the paper with an awl to make the lines stand out on the gold without damaging it. The areas outside of the design are commonly filled in with dots. Distribute them evenly with consistent pressure and avoid interrupting the geometrical lines that surround them.

• **Designs created with stamping dies**. In this case, you can work through the pattern as you did on the geometric designs, or you can work directly on the gold without damaging it once the paper is removed.

• **Water-colored edges**. After applying the design, scrape off the excess gold with a scalpel in the areas where you plan to apply the watercolors. The result is a series of astonishing contrasts. This technique makes it possible to produce beautiful edges with a few tools in a moderate amount of time, lending the book true artistic value.

▲ Gauffering the edges, and various designs used for that purpose

▲ Moistening the leather before proceeding with tooling

◄ A gauffered edge (by Jordi de la Rica)

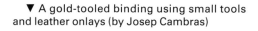

▼ A gold-tooled binding using small tools and leather onlays (by Josep Cambras)

► Tooling with gouges to create an outside border on a binding

Leather Onlays in Bookbinding

Leather onlays make it possible to apply different colored leathers to book covers, resulting in beautiful overall decoration.

Books with leather onlays have existed in the Islamic culture since the 11th century, but it took until the 18th century for this technique to be used in France for the first time. Then it was imitated and modified by various European countries.

Different Types of Onlay Bindings Onlay Designs with Tooling

This oldest onlay technique is one of the most difficult ones to carry out. Only "masters" of gold tooling are successful. After producing the design for the cover or spine of the book, blind tool it as previously described. Once completed, pare down different-colored leathers as much as possible to continue the process.

GOLD TOOLING AN ONLAY

To produce nice gold tooling on an onlay, apply an initial layer of gold leaf after the blind tooling, then immediately attach the onlay, tool it, and then gold tool it a second time. This technique is performed only on highly detailed books because of the extra time it takes. If gold tooling were done only after the onlays were attached, a crack could be seen where the onlay edges appear. Since it is already gold tooled beneath, any irregularity caused by the onlay is totally disguised when it is gold tooled a second time.

• **Hand tooling**. To tool an onlay with decorative hand tools, begin by pasting a piece of paper onto the grain of the pared onlay leather. After it dries, mark the paper with a hand tool on the paper so that it can be cut out exactly. Outline each of its edges. Use scissors to cut out the designs, and submerge them in water so that the onlay leather separates from the paper. While they're drying on a piece of board, scrape the inside of the stamped impressions on your cover with a scalpel so that the pores open up completely. Doing this will assure good adhesion of your onlays. Once the onlay pieces are dry, coat them with paste, and position them in their proper places. With a cold tool, fit them into the design, making sure that they match up well in the impressions. When all the pieces are dry and in place, blind tool them again. Blind tooling can be your final step, or you can gold tool the onlay.

• **With lines and gouges**. This technique is very similar to or the same as using hand tools. Tool the design and then place a piece of thin paper over the cover. Rub it with a soft pencil to transfer the prepared design. From here on, work as you did before; that is, paste it to the onlay leather and go over the design with line pallets and gouges, then cut out the shapes. The design can also be cut out from photocopies of the initial design, although this might not be as precise as an original drawing.

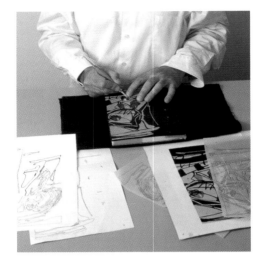

▲ Items for creating bas relief onlay

Leather Decoration by Juxtaposition, or Inlays

Geometrical motifs are commonly used with this type of technique. As usual, first do a drawing on paper to avoid unpleasant surprises later on. You'll be creating a composition from different colors of leather that don't lie on top of the cover but fit together tightly along their edges to form the cover.

Always begin with leathers of the same thickness so that nothing sticks out more than necessary and the book's surface is as uniform as possible.

We've already explained that leather, like other materials, stretches when it is damp and contracts when it dries. It's crucial to the success of your piece that you keep this in mind throughout the process of creating the design.

▼ Onlay decoration (by Josep Cambras)

▼ Onlay binding based on the typography of the manuscript (by Josep Cambras)

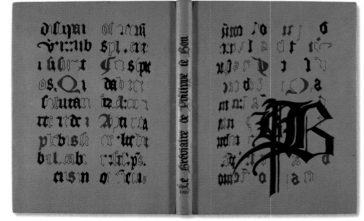

▼ Design created by juxtaposed leathers

▲ Figurative binding using gold tooling and onlays (by Josep Cambras)

To attach the inlays, begin with the spine and continue to the fore edge. Since they'll shrink later, cut the leather pieces slightly larger. Once they're put in place, allow them to dry before trimming. Place the second inlay beside the first, so that no spaces remain between them when they dry. You'll have to force each piece against the other a bit. As the pieces dry, continue with the process. Use your fingertips to fit the next piece to the one that's already dry, trim it, and so on, until you're done.

In instances where there are one or more figures in the center of the cover, cover the book completely with leather before dealing with the inlay. Once it's dry, cut out the areas to be filled and fit the pieces inside.

Bas-Relief Leather Onlays

This simple technique is time-consuming, but it results in very visible and gratifying results for anyone getting started in the world of leather decoration. After experimenting with the bas relief, you'll find an endless number of creative possibilities.

• **Tools and materials**. To experiment with this technique, you'll need a spoon-shaped burin used for leather and tin repoussé. You can buy one at an art supply store. You'll also need some light tracing paper, leathers pared down on the flesh side, and a mixture of PVA and methylcellulose for attaching leather pieces to the book cover.

• **Preparing and creating the onlay**. You'll need a piece of paper or lightweight board the same size as the book covers on which to draw the pieces of your design and color them in rough draft form. To create the original from which you'll work, attach tracing paper to the draft, and use a pencil to draw the outlines of each piece of the design.

Next, assign a number to each leather piece needed and mark the design shape with the corresponding number, based on your rough draft. Make several photocopies of this numbered design, and set them aside for use later. Once the tracing paper is marked, lift it off the rough draft and make sure that all shapes are numbered.

• **Cutting out and attaching the leather pieces**. Take the photocopies that you've set aside, and cut the shapes out in numerical order. Cut outside the initial lines since you'll trim them later to the exact dimensions. To begin this process, overlay the pieces of paper bearing the same number of each matching piece of pared leather. Tape these pieces onto a piece of board in preparation for cutting.

Cut through the two layers with a hobby knife so that the leather pieces come out precisely. Place each piece of leather on the rough draft until the whole design is filled in.

Now you're ready to assemble the onlay. To keep the pieces from getting dirty, place them face down on white paper so the adhesive can be applied using the mixture previously prepared. Use tweezers to position the leather pieces on the book, and press them down lightly with a damp piece of cotton to set them. Remove any excess glue that might be on their edges.

Once the whole assembly is dry, use the heated burin to go over the outlines of the leather pieces. Hold the tool at a slight angle to produce a raised design. When you're done, use an airbrush to apply a layer of watery varnish as a final finish. This coating protects the color of the leathers and gives them a finished sheen.

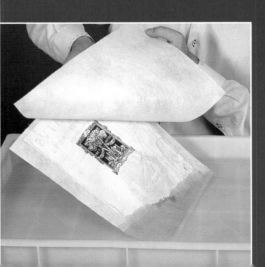

Restoration

*I*n this chapter, we'll address making minor repairs that can be done in a bookbinding workshop. For instance, you might find yourself confronted with a broken cover or an ex libris stuck to a discarded cover that needs rescuing. You might find beautiful bindings that need to be refurbished because they're old or have been treated roughly.

Within this chapter, we've included a chapter on end sheets, because sometimes you'll have to reproduce them using the criterion of the age when the book was bound, while maintaining the same aesthetic spirit in which the book was conceived.

For all these reasons, it's good to have knowledge of these small book problems you may encounter, which can be fixed without having to go to a restorer.

Restoration

Any restorative intervention should be based on the premise of avoiding further damage to the book, both in the present and the future. For this reason, use only harmless products of proven reliability; it's not advisable, for instance, to use self-sticking papers, totally synthetic glues, or any other home-made remedy. In general, before you begin any restoration project, always evaluate whether or not you have the necessary knowledge and materials.

Materials

• **Semi-synthetic adhesive**. Methylcellulose is the easiest-to-find adhesive on the market. Since it is sold in fine granules, it dissolves quickly in cold water.

• **Japanese tissue**. There are many types of Japanese tissue. A fine, lightweight tissue (9–11 grams per square meter) can be used for jobs requiring repairs to rips; and a medium-weight tissue (between 20 and 40 grams per square meter) can be used to repair holes and missing pieces.

• **Protective fabric**. This non-woven polyester fabric is used to protect the leaves and keep the papers from sticking together during the repair process. It is also called polyester web.

• **Brushes, tweezers, spatulas, scissors, scalpels, and weights**. These materials are easy to come by and make it possible to handle projects precisely and cleanly, fulfilling the need for accuracy.

• **Tacking iron**. This tool is used to accelerate the drying process of the repair.

• **Blotting paper**. Used for drying repairs while keeping them flat.

Preparing the Adhesive

Methylcellulose. This harmless, semi-synthetic adhesive is easy to prepare. If used in concentrated form, it is a very strong adhesive. For small projects, it's used in concentration of approximately $2/3$ ounce (20 g) of dry methylcellulose per 1 quart (liter) of water. Keep in mind that the stronger the concentration, the greater the adhesive power, but with stronger versions comes a greater risk of creating shiny spots on the final repair.

◄ Basic materials for small restoration projects

Small Tears and Holes

Use a strip of fine Japanese tissue to repair small tears in pages that result from improper handling. Tear the tissue by hand to a width of about $1/8$ inch (3 mm) and a length slightly greater than the tear. The long fibers at the edges of the torn tissue lend strength to the repair. Straight cuts made with scissors or a scalpel aren't recommended, since they leave no fibers at the edge and are more visible when the process is complete. Apply a strip of Japanese tissue on the side of the page where it will have the least effect on the text or illustrations and where it will blend in best.

First, place a piece of protective fabric behind the page on which you're working. Then use a brush to apply a thin, uniform layer of adhesive about $1/32$ inch (.8 mm) wide to both sides of the tear. Use tweezers to set the strip of Japanese tissue in place; it has to cover the tear completely and stick out over the edges. Overlay the Japanese tissue with another piece of protective cloth, and dry it with the aid of a tacking iron.

In instances where you need to cover holes made by insects, use Japanese tissue of a weight similar to that of the page (two layers can be applied if necessary). Proceed in a similar fashion: first of all, mark the shape of the hole on the Japanese tissue, and tear it with your hands or the tweezers, about $1/32$ inch (.8 mm) larger than the outline on all sides. Apply adhesive all around the edge of the hole, and after setting the piece in place, dry it with the tacking iron.

To create color in the Japanese tissue similar to that of the pages, dye the tissue. You can use natural products such as coffee, tea, and chamomile, which produce, respectively, shades of dark brown, light brown, and yellow. Use a saline solution as a mordant.

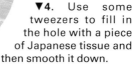

◄▼ **1 and 2**. Apply adhesive to both edges of the tear, and place the strip of Japanese tissue over it.

▼**3**. Dry the strip with a low-temperature tacking iron. To avoid touching the japanese tissue, insert a piece of protective cloth between the iron and the paper. Move the tool gently to keep it from sticking.

▼**4**. Use some tweezers to fill in the hole with a piece of Japanese tissue and then smooth it down.

Separated Leaves

To repair separated leaves, use long strips of torn Japanese tissue as if you're dealing with a normal tear. Apply the paper to the outside of the signature fold to make it much stronger when it's folded. A similar process is done to form new signatures from single pages or sheets.

▲ Join the two pages with a strip of Japanese tissue, using the same technique that you would to repair a tear.

▲ Papers of various origin used in restoration

Cleaning Book Spines

To clean book spines, prepare a thicker adhesive than usual (about 1.1 ounces [30 grams] per quart [liter]). Apply a layer to the entire surface of the spine, leaving it for a short while under plastic film until the older glue softens.

Use light pressure with a spatula to remove the glue. If the glue does not come off the entire surface, repeat the operation until the spine is clean and the threads and bands can be cut for taking the book apart. (This operation is not possible if the glue is synthetic because it is irreversible.)

▶ **1.** Pasting up the spine with methylcellulose to soften the existing glue, which is covered with a strip of plastic film to retard drying

▼ **2.** When the glue has softened, remove the plastic film used to prevent drying, and scrape the spine carefully with a scalpel or spatula.

Lifting the Ex Libris and Endsheets

In order to lift an ex libris (bookplate) or other paper adhered to the surface of a leaf, you must first find out if the inks are soluble. If they aren't, place the page between two sheets of protective fabric in a bath of hot water about 104° F (40° C).

After a few minutes, the adhesive should soften. Before the water cools off, gently remove the stuck paper with the aid of a brush. Let it dry on a flat surface on sheets of protective fabric, and once it's dry, give it a coating of methylcellulose in a solution of about 2/3 ounce (20 g) per quart (liter) right where it sits.

◀ **1.** Placing the papers into the bath on an angle to avoid forming bubbles

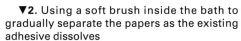

▼**2.** Using a soft brush inside the bath to gradually separate the papers as the existing adhesive dissolves

Restoring Antique Bindings

◄ Some of the most common binding defects that need restoration

W hat you've already read about repairing paper in books can serve as a beginning to this section. Among the most common cases you're likely to encounter are damaged spines, damaged corners, loose boards, and missing pieces of leather on the boards. Always spend enough time doing an initial study of the problem to save time and figure out the best point at which to begin the restoration.

Damaged Spines

In bookbinding there was a change in binding techniques beginning in the second third of the 19th century. For this reason, you may find two different possibilities for broken spines: one in which the spine's leather is still glued to the body of the book but has lost some pieces; and another in which the entire spine has come loose from the binding.

In the first case, remove the old spine of the book. For this you'll need a scalpel to detach the spine without damaging the leather.

Do this with the greatest care, since the dried leather can break like glass. At the same time, proceed with caution to avoid damaging the signatures and the sewing, since, during this time period, the leather was glued directly to the spine of the textblock.

Once the spine is separated, set it aside for use later on. Beginning at this point, the steps to follow are basically the same in both cases, but there's enough latitude to vary them as you deem necessary.

Since the boards are still held to the book by the original cord attachment, you must lift the leather slightly from the board near the spine while keeping the boards in place to insert new leather underneath it. Use the scalpel and proceed as explained previously.

Cut out a new spine separately from lightweight board, and attach it to the book. Cover it with leather and leave the turn-ins loose. Using paste and a bone folder, insert the turn-ins underneath the original leather. Place the book between sheets of protective fabric, and squeeze it in the press to assure total adhesion. Thus, you have a book with a new leather spine to serve as a support for the original spine that you set aside previously.

To attach it to the new leather, sand the edges of the old spine down as thinly as possible, and apply adhesive so it can be attached at the appropriate place. In order to avoid an unsuccessful attachment, wrap the book tightly and set aside to dry.

Once it is dry, remove the wrap, and if necessary, tint any parts that need to blend in the repair.

▼ In some cases, it's necessary to reproduce bindings with tooling as close as possible to the original (by Josep Cambras).

▲ **1.** Attaching a new piece of leather to serve as a support for the original spine

▲ **2.** Attaching the old spine

◄ **3.** Wrapping the book with a bandage to make the spine adhere completely

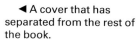

▶ Reinforce the inside of the gutter with a piece of Japanese paper.

◀ A cover that has separated from the rest of the book.

Damaged Corner Pieces

If the corner pieces of a book have been hit, give them a few light blows with a mallet, and stiffen them up with some glue to restore them.

If material, whether leather or cardboard, is missing from the corner, the process is more complicated. In this case, lift the piece of damaged leather up and use the paper cutter to cut the ends of the cardboard that are in bad condition. Fit a new piece of cardboard of the same thickness to the corner. Glue it at the joint, and reinforce the top and bottom with a piece of porous paper.

When it's dry, the missing piece of leather or paper must be superimposed, and it should be as similar to the original as possible. When that's done, install the old leather over the new and sand down the ends to disguise the thickness.

▲ 1. This photo shows an older binding that has lost a portion of a corner.

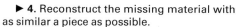

▲ 2. After lifting the paper from the cover as much as possible, cut away the original board, and position a new corner piece.

◀ 3. Glue the new piece on at the butt edge. Adhere a piece of paper to each side to reinforce it.

▶ 4. Reconstruct the missing material with as similar a piece as possible.

Missing Pieces of Leather

Many times, in addition to spine and corner pieces in poor condition, the cover panels are also creased or missing material. These bindings might have great historical value, so it's worth the trouble to preserve them and spend the time reconstructing them.

One of the steps that can be taken is to lift up the leather to install another piece underneath it, neaten up the edges, and put it back in place. Depending on the nature of the damage, this is an option to consider.

Another solution is to make a paste using hide trimmings and paste. To do this, chop up the leather and boil it in water. Once a more or less homogeneous mass is formed, mix the paste in and cover the holes with this mixture. When it's dry, color it in a way that's similar to the rest of the book, and then apply wax all over it.

Marbled Papers

This is an old technique of decorating paper that involves floating the colors on the surface of a gelatinous liquid so that they are transferable to paper or another material. Papers used for marbling should be pretreated with alum, which serves as a mordant to help the color to adhere.

These papers originated in the Orient. Beginning in the 16th century, merchants brought them to the West. They were referred to as "Turkish marble" because of their resemblance to the veins in marble.

Materials

- **Colors and gelatins**. A variety of colors and gelatins with different properties are available for marbling.
- **A basin**. Choose one that's 2 to 3 inches deep (5.1 to 7.6 cm) to hold the prepared liquid, and slightly over 1 inch (2.5 cm) larger than the paper on each side.
- **Round containers**. These are used in preparing the colors.
- **Brushes**. These are used to remove the color and splatter it onto the gelatin.
- **Dropper**. A dropper is used to measure the ox gall and to put the color on the gelatin.
- **Stick**. You can strike a brush against a stick so the color splatters onto the gelatin in small droplets.
- **Small sticks or needles**. These are used for applying color or for "drawing" the color.
- **Combs**. Made up of "teeth" arranged at various distances apart, combs are used to create patterns on the surface of the gelatin.
- **Strips of newspaper.** Keep this material on hand for cleaning and eliminating any impurities from the surface of the gelatin before applying the colors.
- **Papers**. Diverse papers can be used for marbling, but porous ones weighing between 80 and 120 grams are always preferable.

The Gelatin

This liquid base that holds the color on the surface comes in different densities that effect the marbling results. Various products are used for thickening water, such as gum tragacanth, methylcellulose, and carrageenan. We'll concentrate on explaining how to prepare the gelatin with the marine algae known as Chondus crispus, which is

▲ Various types of marbled papers or "Turkish marble"

easy to find in natural food stores under the name of carrageenan or Irish moss.

The approximate ratio is 2 ounces per quart of water (12.5 g / l). To prepare it, bring part of the water to a boil. Then add the algae and allow the mixture to cook for 10 minutes.

Then turn off the heat and add the rest of the cold water before straining it. Stir it from time to time during the next 24 hours. At about 64° F (18° C) the gelatin will keep well for a week without preservatives, but it loses its properties with time and in response to the ambient temperature.

The Colors

Various coloring media can be used for marbling, such as oils, temperas, and acrylics. Oily colors, such as oil and typographic inks, merely need to be mixed with turpentine to make them float on the gelatin.

On the other hand, water-based colors, such as tempera and acrylics, have to be diluted with distilled water to form a light, homogenous cream. Then ox gall is added to them, which is insoluble in water, causing them to float on the surface, spread out, and keep the colors from mixing together. The quantity of ox gall that you add varieIf you use this logic, you can add more colors until the surface is covered, without exceeding the limits of the paper's absorption. It's a good

▶ **1.** Once the color is ready, spread it on the gelatin in a pattern of your choice.

▼ **2.** Use a wood stick to splatter small droplets of color.

▼ **3.** Dropping color onto the gelatin with a brush is another way to create a pattern.

▲ **4.** Colors spread out on the gelatin

▲ **5.** Using a stick to draw out the color

▲ **6.** Combing the whole surface after drawing out the color

idea to test the dilation of drops in different colors on the gelatin, keeping in mind that the more ox gall you add, the greater the drops expand.

Marbling

Begin by adding the colors to the gelatin with a loaded brush, allowing the drops to fall with a slight movement. Then, strike the brush against a stick, or drop the paint on the surface with an eyedropper or a needle. When the drops cover the entire gelatin, they form a marble or "stone" pattern.

To create patterns, pass a stick from side to side on the gelatin to form lines referred to as drawn marble. Then, if you wish, pass a comb from top to bottom and perpendicular to the lines in the drawn marble. These designs are known as comb or nonpareil marble, and they vary with the comb used, whether spike, cluster, or another type of comb. If you randomly mix the drops all over the surface, the result is what's known as "waters." Stretch the drops, press them against each other, or spread them out, and they can be manipulated to form an intentional design, whether abstract or figurative.

Once the design is finished, transfer it to the paper. Hold the paper at an angle and begin placing it on the surface on one side or a corner. Place it on the gelatin with great care to avoid air bubbles. When the entire paper is resting on top of the gelatin, move it back and forth slightly to form lighter and darker shadows known as folding or shading.

Next, lift the paper with your fingertips and lightly support it on the basin's edge, drawing

it upward so it touches and eliminates as much gelatin as possible from the paper's surface. The marbling and design from the gelatin will be mirrored on the paper. Hang up the paper or leave it flat to dry, then press it to make it smooth.

Depending on the texture of the gelatin, the colors, and the order in which they're used. Carefully add it to the color without letting air bubbles form. If the combination is right, a drop will float on the gelatinous surface and make a circle about 2 inches (5 cm) across.

The amount of ox gall that you add to the color creates a certain pressure. It keeps the colors separated, but too much of it will cause problems with your design. The order in which the colors are used also depends on the quantity of ox gall each color contains. That is, the first drops will expand to full size; drops containing more gall will push against these as they expand; and the third ones will require more gall than the second to expand.

▶ **7.** Placing the paper on the gelatin

▶ **8.** Cleaning off the paper on the edge of the basin

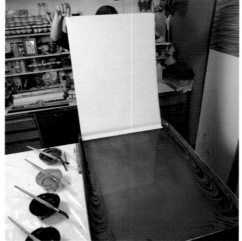

*T*his chapter contains a series of illustrated exercises summarizing basic bookbinding construction. We've already explained most of these techniques throughout the course of the book. From among many possibilities, we've chosen eight because of their diversity and complementary technical nature. Use these exercises as a guide, and with hours of practice and experimentation, you can apply them to various projects made with various kinds of material.

Bookbinding
Exercises

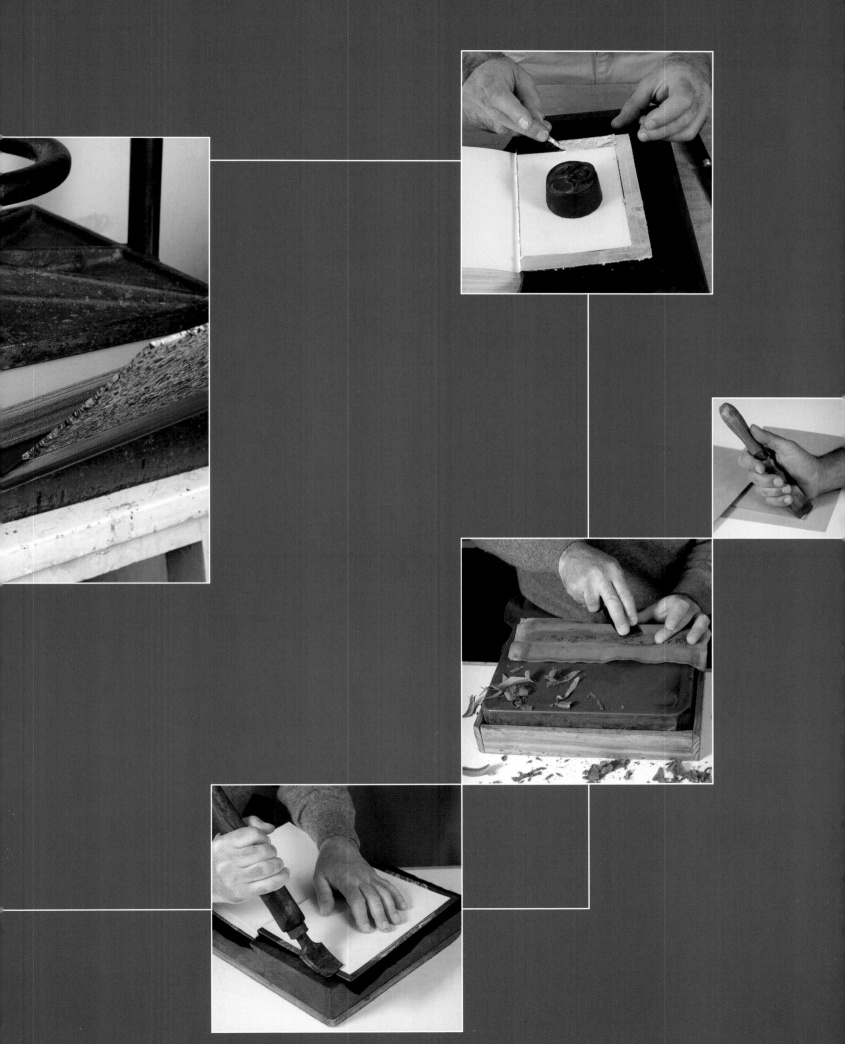

Binding in Cloth

*T*his type of binding has a simple cased structure, but it's possible to use a great variety of materials and decorative applications within this framework. Even though cloth binding is somewhat plain, don't underestimate its value; it is nearly impossible to learn other structures correctly if you don't master this one first.

▲ **1.** After the book is disbound, its pages repaired, and the paper covers hinged, you can proceed with the sawing. The saw-kerfs must correspond to the number and position of the desired sewing cords and be exactly the right depth to reach the inner folio of each signature.

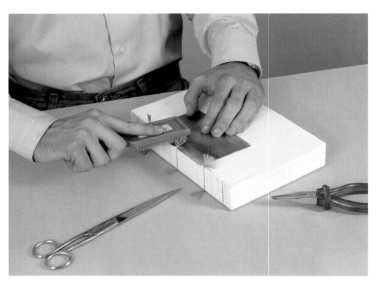

▲ **2.** Once the book is sewn together, use a mallet to reduce the swelling, and cut the cord extensions slightly more than ¹/2 inch (1.3 cm) long. Fray them uniformly so they all have the same thickness.

◀ **3.** Cut the end sheets to the precise dimensions of the book and tip them, flush to the head, at the back edge of the first and last signatures. Avoid getting spots on the pages.

◀ **4.** Paste the cords down onto the end sheets, and smooth them out to avoid lumps.

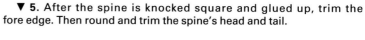

▼ **5.** After the spine is knocked square and glued up, trim the fore edge. Then round and trim the spine's head and tail.

▲ **6.** Backing must be done carefully, keeping your shoulder height uniform as you work.

▲ **7.** Use a fine layer of adhesive to attach the endbands and mull. Apply it from the middle toward the ends to avoid getting it onto the book's trimmed edges and end sheets.

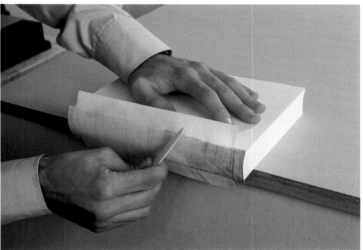

▲ **8.** When attaching the endbands and mull, the mull shouldn't go over the endbands and should extend equally on both sides of the spine.

▶ **9.** Attach the paper lining with a third gluing. This has to form a hollow tube on the spine to facilitate the opening of the book.

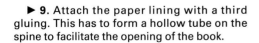

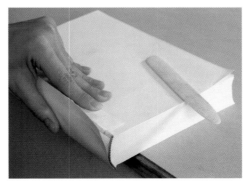

▶ **10.** Remove the excess part of the hollow that is flush with the last signature.

◄ **11.** Once the boards for the covers and the lightweight board for the spine strip are cut out, cut the cloth so it extends about $1/2$ inch (1.3 cm) on each side. Then, paste up the cloth.

▼ **12.** Place the boards and spine strip on the cloth, leaving about $1/4$ inch (6 mm) between them. Cut each of the corners, and assemble the cover.

▲ **13.** Hold the cover vertically on the counter, turn the cloth in with your thumbs (always from the outside to inside), and pull it tight so there are no air pockets or bubbles.

▼ **14.** Use the spine former to round the spine strip uniformly, beginning at one end and finishing at the other. Make it slightly rounder than the book's spine so it fits tightly.

▼ **15.** Apply adhesive to the spine, and place the book on one board, applying pressure with your hand so that the spine adheres to the book. Before the adhesive dries completely, adjust the positioning for even squares as needed.

◄ **16.** Once the covers are attached, use a bone folder to rub the joints of the book down.

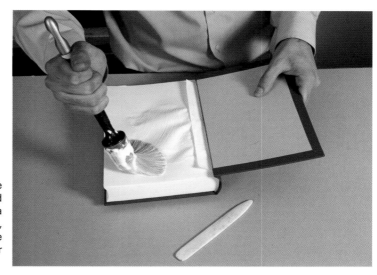

► **17.** Once the spine is dry, paste the end sheets down. Use a fairly thin adhesive, and always move the brush from the center toward the outside.

◄ **18.** Once the end sheets are pasted down, place the book between two boards, and put it into the press for a few seconds. Then, take it out to make certain it's properly adhered, and no glue has squeezed out.

► **19.** Leave it weighted down for 24 hours. The book is then ready to be stamped with the appropriate title.

Half-Leather Binding with Raised Bands

*J*ust as clothbound books are the basis for any book with a cased structure, binding in half leather, or "Dutch" binding, is the basis for all kinds of bound (attached-board) structures. In addition, if you add raised bands and corners, you'll have the prerequisites for a variety of styles. Because of the way the boards are attached directly to the sewing structure, this type of binding is more solid in finished form and allows the covers to open more easily.

▲ **1.** To prepare a book with a bound structure for sewing, the paper covers should be hinged (if they are present), the end leaves must be reinforced with linen, and two more leaves should be added to them to make up false end papers.

▲ **2.** Once the book is sewn, trim it. Avoid gluing the cords to the end leaf because you'll need them later for attaching the boards. The boards must be laminated, as shown in the photograph, with another piece of binders' board or lightweight board.

◄ **3.** Make the shoulders the same thickness as the laminated boards, then cut out the boards that make up the covers. Once they're cut out, use a paring knife or some other implement to back-corner them.

▼ **4.** Mark a line with a pencil near the board's edge indicating the areas you'll bevel on three sides. Use a rasp to bevel the boards, followed by sandpaper.

▼ **5.** Attach the frayed cords to the board with paste, then smooth them out with the bone folder so they don't form lumps.

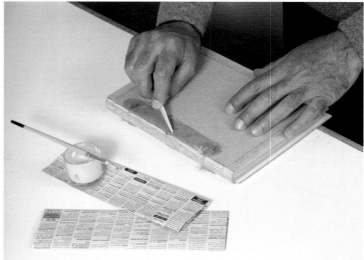

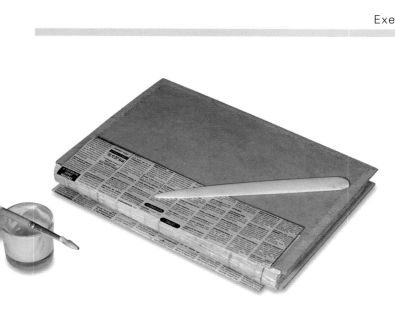
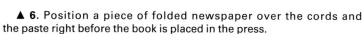

▲ **6.** Position a piece of folded newspaper over the cords and the paste right before the book is placed in the press.

▲ **7.** Place the book between boards, including the spine, and allow it to remain under heavy pressure in the press for 24 hours. The cords will sink into the board and form a compact unit.

▶ **8.** Once the book is dry, take it out of the press and pull off the excess newspaper. Use the bone folder to adjust the shoulders to the thickness of the boards, and go over the cords to remove any lumps.

▶ **9.** When you apply adhesive to the spine, attach the endbands and mull, which should span from the first to the last signature (shoulder to shoulder) without reaching beyond either one.

▼ **10.** Apply the paper liner in the same way, this time without a hollow tube. The liner must span from the first to last signature and extend past the endbands. Because of the adhesive, it will be more stable.

▼ **11.** Once the spine dries, remove any excess paper and adhesive. Smooth it with sandpaper before attaching the lightweight board.

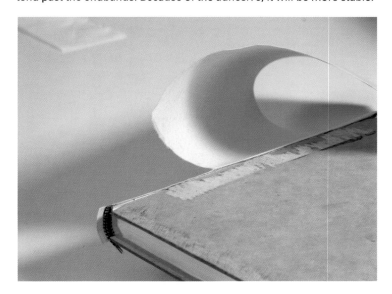

◀ **12.** After a first strip of lightweight board is attached to the spine at the side edges, coat it with adhesive so a second strip (already marked with the location of the false raised bands) can be added.

▶ **13.** Smooth the second piece of lightweight board with sandpaper to eliminate any lumps.

◀ **14.** Cut the leather to dimension before beginning to pare the edges. Mark the joints and thin them with sandpaper by folding back the leather at the joint and sanding a groove.

▶ **15.** Cut the corners out in the same way as the leather for the spine, and pare them in the usual way. Set them aside until you're ready to attach them.

◀ **16.** Once the joints are sanded, use the paring knife to thin the spine area between them. Next, stretch the leather carefully over the edge of the table to improve its flexibility.

◀ **17.** False raised bands are attached using strips of leather positioned in proportion to the size and thickness of the volume.

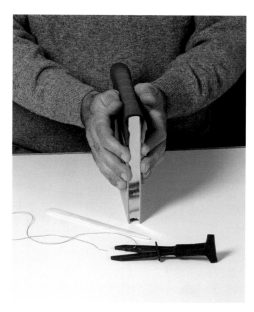

◀ **18.** Once the pasted leather is centered on the spine, pull it down over it with the palms of your hands and the base of your thumbs. This will help the leather stretch evenly onto the sides of the book without it getting damaged.

▶ **19.** Tightening the raised bands with the band nippers for the first time. Later, you'll return to this step for the final finish.

▲ **20.** Use your thumbs to pull the boards back away from the spine so the turn-ins can be made at the head and tail. Avoid getting the edges and the endbands dirty.

▲ **21.** Use the bone folder to stretch the leather with the help of thread placed in the back corners of the boards.

▶ **22.** Place a piece of lightweight board flush with the edges of the covers, and use the bone folder to set the endcap. Make sure that it's centered evenly between the boards, and that it forms a half-moon shape at the cap.

▶ **23.** Once the leather on the spine is dry, place the corners. Paste them and position them evenly on the book.

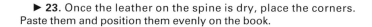

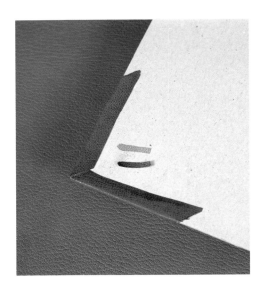

◄ **24.** Turn the corners without overlapping the leather at the corner. Finish them off with a small piece of leather thinned down and cut to the right size.

► **25.** To attach the lightweight board fill-ins for the sides, place them on the sides before folding them in. Then mark and cut them.

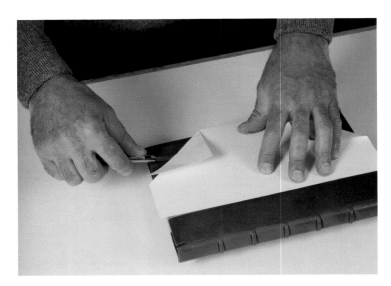

◄ **26.** Use the burnisher to mark the leather on a previously marked line, creating a "step" into which the edge of the paper sides can be placed.

► **27.** When trimming the sides at the corners, you can make the inside cut with a straightedge and hobby knife.

▼ **28.** Attach the sides once you've applied the adhesive. Make certain that the paper matches up perfectly with the burnished mark on the leather.

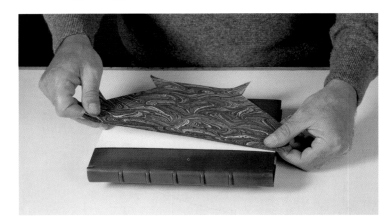

► **29.** After trimming out the interior with a ruler and a pair of dividers, cut out liners to the exact size as the inside space, taking the paper's expansion after pasting into consideration. After you attach the liners, place the book in the press for 24 hours.

▼ **30.** Once it's out of the press, clean the leather with a mixture of water and vinegar, and allow it to dry. Then burnish the turn-ins. Remove the false end papers and any leftover adhesive from the back.

▲**31.** Cut out the previously prepared end sheets using a template made to the exact size.

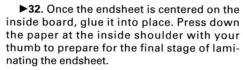

►**32.** Once the endsheet is centered on the inside board, glue it into place. Press down the paper at the inside shoulder with your thumb to prepare for the final stage of laminating the endsheet.

► **33.** After leaving the book in the press for 24 hours with a piece of lightweight board between the end sheets, trim them to the size of the book. This last step finishes the book.

A Portfolio with Flaps for Graphic Works

*T*he *portfolio shown here, based on the conventional one with ties, is one of many variations you can choose to protect any kind of document or graphic work. The flaps protect the enclosed document from light and dust, keeping out potentially harmful external elements. Naturally, there's no title on the spine; a binder's title or label on the front panel identifies the contents. These portfolios are stored horizontally inside drawers or on bookshelves.*

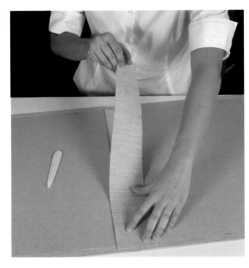

◀ **2.** Once the boards are attached to the fabric with an appropriate distance between them for making the spine, line the inside spine with a strip of the same cloth that extends over each side and onto the boards.

▲ **1.** Cut out the materials to dimension for making the portfolio and its accompanying flaps.

▲ **3.** Next, attach some liners to the inside to prevent future warping.

▲ **4.** Cover the front flap, leaving the longest cloth extension unturned, since it will be held in place later underneath the lining.

▲ **5.** Cover the outside of the side flaps, leaving the lower part unturned.

◀ **6.** Once covered, use the same flap of the portfolio as a template for cutting out the cloth to be attached to the inside.

▶ **7.** Once the cloth is cut for the inside, apply paste to it, and attach it evenly on all sides.

◄ **8.** Once the flaps are covered, use a pencil to mark where the hinge will fold on both the outside and inside. Make this mark the same distance from the edge on all three flaps.

► **9.** Cut lightweight board to provide pastedowns for the portfolio. Cover the exterior and turn it in. This photo shows the flap and how to adhere it along the marked line under the lightweight board, which is nipped in the press to assure total adhesion.

◄ **10.** Use a hobby knife to make a cut in the side to accommodate the ties. Glue them down to the liner inside the portfolio cover.

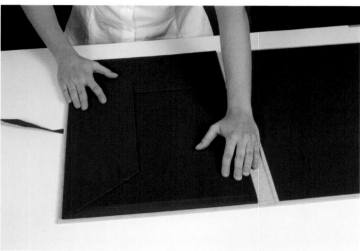

► **11.** Attaching the pastedowns with the flaps already attached to one of them.

▲ **12.** Once the pastedowns are attached, keep them weighted until they're dry to avoid possible warping later on.

► **13.** Once the portfolio is completely dry, it is ready to hold documents.

A Drop-spine Tray

*A*ll boxes serve a protective function, since they're used to preserve their contents. A drop-spine tray does more than beautify the library; its primary purpose is functional because it protects its contents from external elements such as light and dust. These boxes are relatively easy to make and very useful.

▲ **1.** Cut out three edge pieces the same thickness as the book; you'll trim the length later on. Cut the tray's base as wide as the book plus the thickness of one board, and the same height of the book plus the thickness of two boards. In addition, add about $1/32$ inch (.8 mm) to both dimensions to allow room for the attached cloth.

▲ **2.** Once the base is cut out, you'll attach the edge pieces (walls). Cut one to the length of the base, and cut the two sides to the dimensions of the width of the base, minus the thickness of one board. Once everything is trimmed to size, assemble it as shown in the photograph.

▲ **3.** After you've assembled the first, or smaller tray, you'll use this tray as the basis for the larger tray, using the same procedure that you did to make the small tray based on the book. Once the second tray is assembled, cut out the spine, making it as wide as the thickness of that tray and the same height.

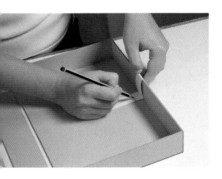

▲ **4.** Once everything is in place, cut out the cloth. Use strips of paper to figure out the measurements—the height is the same as that of the large tray base, plus four times the width of the edge piece, plus about 1 $1/2$ inches (3.8 cm). To determine the width of the cloth, add together the width of the spine and four times the width of the larger tray edge piece, plus about 2 inches (5 cm).

▲ **5.** After cutting out the cloth, center the two trays and spine on it, leaving a joint space of two board thicknesses between each tray and spine. Make a pencil outline of the three parts on the cloth before applying the paste.

▲ **6.** Once the cloth is pasted, place the parts in their correct positions.

► **7.** Make the cuts as indicated in the photograph, using a hobby knife on top of a piece of scrap board. For the fore edge flaps, it's best to use a ruler, since the cut has to be slightly tangential to the edge of the base.

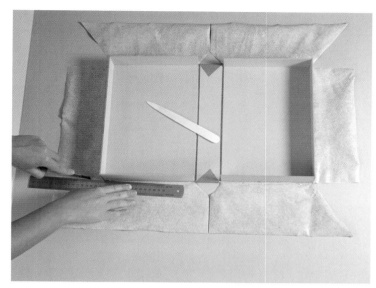

►**8.** Turn in the cloth on the top and bottom parts first. The cut shown here helps to bring the top and bottom flaps inside and over the corner.

◄ **9.** The cut on this part of the tray follows the edge of the board so the whole wall is covered when it's turned inside the tray. (If the cloth dries out during this process, give it a second coat of adhesive.)

► **10.** Once the outside of the box is covered, attach a liner to the base of each tray. Cut out the final inside lining as long as the open case and as wide as the inside of the large tray. Once it is cut out to size, make a step in the cloth so it fits the inside of the small tray.

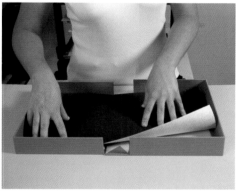

▲ **11.** Once it's cut to proper dimensions, make sure it fits well inside before adhering it, taking into account the fact that it might expand.

► **12.** Don't use too much adhesive, since it can squeeze out and mar the inside of the box. Also, fit the cloth down into the joints with your fingers so the box will close properly.

Slipcase Edged in Leather

This is one of the most common kinds of enclosures used in binding. It can be used to protect the sides of the finished bindings from possible scratches as well as protect older bindings and keep their covers in place. On older bindings, the leather can dry out and break along the spine if there isn't support to keep the boards in place.

This type of case protects the book, while allowing the rich spine decoration to show.

▲ **1.** Materials laid out for making the slipcase: binders' board, lightweight board, paper or cloth for lining the inside, and strips of pared leather.

▲**2.** Use two boards for the side panels that are slightly larger than the book and will be cut to size later. The three edge pieces should be as wide as the book is thick. First, apply adhesive to the lightweight board and laminate it along a pencil-drawn line about 1/4 inch (6 mm) from the edge of each side panel.

▼ **3.** Coat the material for the slipcase's lining with adhesive, and position it on top of the lightweight board. The small bit of extra material at the front can be sanded off later. Line the edge pieces in the same way, directly onto the board.

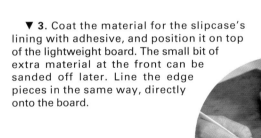

◄ **4.** Before the adhesive dries, use the bone folder to define the "step" produced by the lightweight board on the binders' board.

► **5.** Trimming the board pieces to size is an important step. The side panels should be as high as the book plus the thickness of two edge pieces, and the same width as the book from the point of the curvature (shoulder) on the spine plus the thickness of one edge piece. With respect to the edge pieces, the one that is placed at the fore edge should be as high as the panels of the slipcase, but the edge pieces at the tail and head should measure the same as the entire width of the book. Round one end of each to match the book's spine curvature.

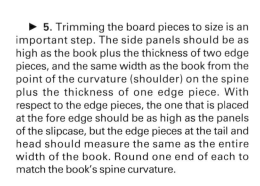

▲ **6.** Sand the exposed outside edge of the slipcase panels to a 45° angle in a slightly rounded shape, as well as the 3/4 inch (1.9 cm) of the edge pieces that are in line with this shape.

▲ **7.** If possible, use a mixture of paste and PVA to coat the leather.

▲ **8.** To attach the leather for the head and tail edge pieces, center them about 1/4 inch (6 mm) from the edge, turned over the edge, and stretched tightly from the ends to mold over the round shape.

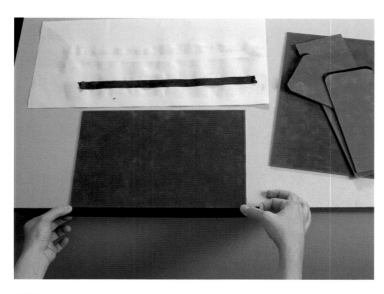

◄ **9.** To install the strips for the panels, attach the pasted leather into the step produced by the lightweight board.

► **10.** Once that's attached, trim the strips flush with the edges of the panels at the step only, leaving the rest so it can be turned back onto the outside of the panels and edge pieces.

◄ **11.** Turn the leather onto the outside of the slipcase panels.

► **12.** Once the leather is dry, run the burnisher over the inner and outer surfaces to improve the finish.

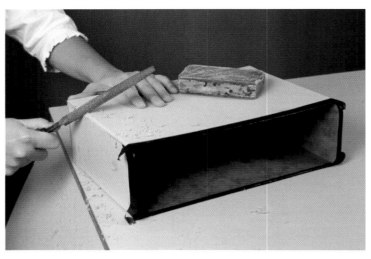

▲ **13.** Now that the pieces are cut to the correct dimensions, you'll assemble the slipcase in the usual way. First, attach the edge pieces to one panel, and then attach the other panel on top of them. If necessary, use tape to hold it together until the adhesive is completely dry.

▲ **14.** Once the slipcase is dry, use a rasp to bevel the six remaining edges, which, like the opening, must be at a slightly rounded 45° angle.

► **15.** Use a piece of sandpaper to finish the four edges of each panel so they have the same angle.

► **16.** Cut off the leather extensions on the panel edges at an angle in relation to the board. Paste the remaining bit onto the sides of the head and tail.

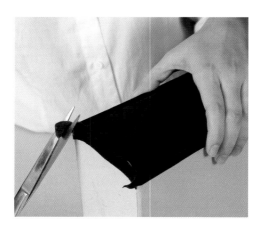

▼ **17.** Use a ruler and hobby knife to trim the leather evenly on the panels. Once that's done, cover the edge pieces with cloth to reinforce them.

▼ **18.** To create the same thickness as the cloth and leather, fill in the area with a piece of lightweight board.

▼ **19.** Cut out the paper for the panels, and attach it at about 3/16 inch (5 mm) from the edge of the opening when folding onto the edge pieces, place them as close together as possible without overlapping them. Make the cuts as indicated in the photograph.

► **20.** Attach the three paper edge pieces, beginning with the upper and lower edges and finishing with the back edge piece, which will be trimmed to the same length as the slipcase.

▲ **21.** Fill the inside of the slipcase with rags to expand the panels slightly. Then wrap the whole slipcase with cloth bandages to prevent the opening from warping outward. After it dries, it appears slightly convex because of the rounded edges.

► **22.** Remove the wrapping and rags from inside the slipcase. Insert the book and weight the whole assembly for 24 hours. The slipcase is then finished, with a slight curvature toward the outside center, in contrast to the heavier look of most slipcases of this type.

A Drop-spine Box with a Rounded Spine in Quarter Leather

In this exercise you'll learn how to make this box in quarter leather, but it is also possible to make one in full leather or parchment, since the structural procedure is the same. This type of enclosure keeps the book totally protected inside, and the outside of it can be embellished with all sorts of decorative finishes, just like a book. It can be used to hold old books and documents, whether for preserving them or dignifying their contents.

▲ **1.** First of all, make two trays that fit together, as you would for a simple drop-spine box. Cover them separately in cloth, without joining them at the spine. Once the trays are covered, cut out the boards for the cover about ¹/8 inch (3 mm) larger per side (head, tail, and fore edge) than the larger tray.

▲**2.** A photo of the completed trays as they look after they've been covered inside and out.

◄ **3.** Cut a piece of lighweight board the same length as the large tray and the same width as the thickness of the tray, plus the thickness of two boards. Attach this board to the bottom of a piece of wood in a half-round shape the same length and slightly narrower than the board. Then adhere a rounded and previously beveled piece of lightweight board to the wooden spine, as shown in the photograph.

►**4.** To provide more strength, adhere a second piece of lightweight board with beveled edges to the first one. To line this spine of wood and lightweight board, cut out and adhere a piece of fabric larger than its base.

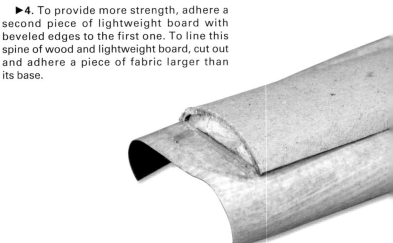

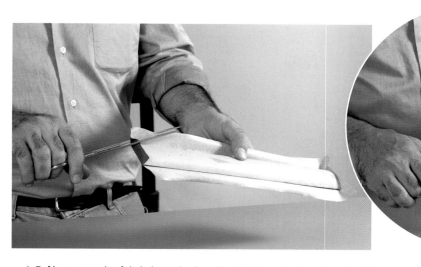

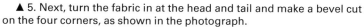

◄ 6. Don't overlap the fabric at the ends. Use scissors to cut it flush with the curve at the head and tail.

▼ 7. Once the cloth is cut, attach the endbands.

▲ 5. Next, turn the fabric in at the head and tail and make a bevel cut on the four corners, as shown in the photograph.

▼ 8. Next, cut out a piece of lightweight board that is the width of the entire curvature of the spine you've already made and as long as the cover boards. With the leather pared, assemble the covers, leaving a 5/64-inch (2 mm) joint space between the lightweight board and the boards.

▼ 9. While the leather is still soft, adhere the rigid spine to the lightweight board spine.

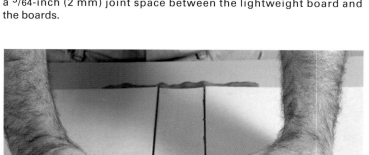

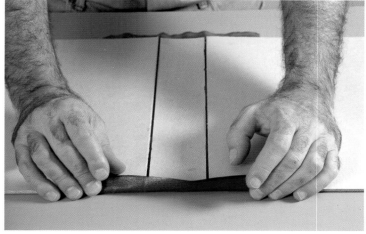

◄ 10. Stretch the cover a bit for the spine to fit in while the leather is still moist.

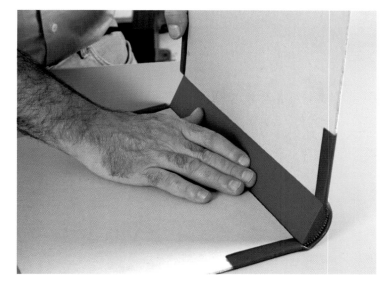

► 11. After the spine is assembled, place the trays in their correct position. Next, you'll make the endcaps as if you're working with a book.

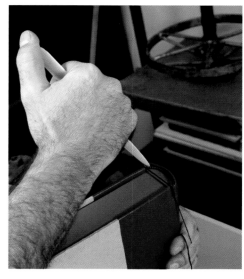

► **12.** Hold the lightweight board in place for forming the endcap.

► **13.** After using the bone folder, the endcap looks like this.

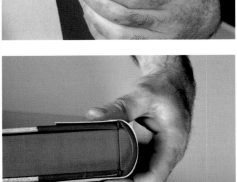

▲ **14.** Once the assembly is dry, cut out a cloth spine lining slightly shorter and wider than the spine's interior so it can be attached over the spine piece and onto the cover boards, 3/4 inch (1.9 cm) per side. Adhere it and rub it down with a bone folder on the inside joints.

► **15.** Cut the corners of the cloth spine lining at an angle.

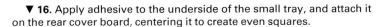

▼ **16.** Apply adhesive to the underside of the small tray, and attach it on the rear cover board, centering it to create even squares.

► **17.** Cut out several pieces of board to fit inside the tray so it can be placed in the press without damaging the walls. Mount the board under the rear cover as well, to protect the rounded spine from damage.

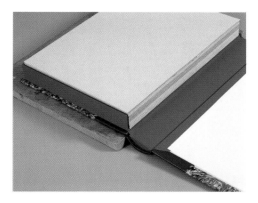

▲ **18.** Repeat this process with the other tray. After applying adhesive to the underside of the large tray, fit it over the small tray, and then close the cover carefully, making sure that the two trays fit together perfectly. Open it flat again to fill it in and press the large tray onto the front cover.

▲ **19.** The tray opens like a book, while serving its purpose of storing and protecting a book or document.

◀ **20.** This exterior view of the tray shows that it has the same appearance as a book in quarter leather.

Gold Tooling the Turn-ins and Board Edge

*W*e've already explored gilding with gold leaf, and this more detailed technique uses a set of rolls to create a unified design on the inside edge of the cover.

By forming a gilded frame around them, this kind of decoration sets off the printed pages when a reader is leafing through the book. The fillet or double-fillet line on the edge of the boards lends it an ethereal air, since it counteracts the board's heaviness. This decoration is found on both classical bindings with sumptuous gilding on their covers as well as Jansenist bindings with the decoration inside.

▲ **1.** Once the book is dry and the liners attached, apply a light layer of paste thinned with water to the inside turn-ins.

▲ **2.** Use a piece of cotton dipped in vinegar to remove any residual paste. Next, run a dry piece of cotton over the inside edge to polish it.

▼ **3.** Use the burnisher along the turn-ins to create a higher polish. If the leather is still a bit damp, there's danger of darkening it.

▲ **4.** Do a trial run of designs made with rolls on a piece of paper. Use a pair of dividers to measure the roll that goes on the outside, and mark a line with the bone folder as a guideline for the fillet.

▲ **5.** Use a fine brush to apply two or three coats of egg glaire to the leather, depending on how porous it is. Wait for each coat to dry before applying the next.

◄ 6. While the glaire is drying, gather all the necessary items around you to continue the process. Cut the gold leaf into strips.

▼ 7. Use short strokes to moisten the inside edge with sweet almond oil in preparation for attaching the gold leaf.

► 8. Use nothing but the natural oils on your fingers to pick up the gold. Here, we're using a double leaf.

► 9. Apply the gold leaf to the oiled surface, then press down with a small piece of clean cotton to seat it completely.

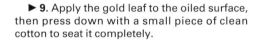

◄ 10. Begin the first fillet on the right. Use the crease that you made earlier with the bone folder (visible through the gold leaf) as a guide.

► 11. When the roll reaches the end, tip it at a 45° angle so it lines up with the adjoining right angle. Repeat this when you reach the other corner.

◄ **12.** Continue tooling the inside edge with the second roll, using the same groove as a guide.

▼ **13.** The rolls gradually form the gold border, joining at the corners.

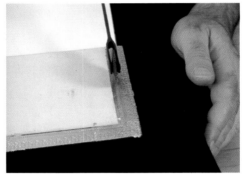

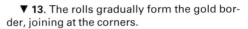

▲ **14.** Go over the fillet or double-fillet lines with a line pallet. At this time, it's preferable to apply a second layer of gold leaf.

► **15.** Pass a thin piece of cotton over the worked surface to easily remove the gold that's not impressed into the leather.

► **16.** Go over it a second time with the same cloth, moistened with a little naptha to remove any particles of gold that may have become impregnated in the leather.

▼ **17.** Once it's clean, pass a heated burnisher over it for the final finish.

▼ **18.** There can be no inside border without outside edge fillet lines, so treat the edges by attaching some gold leaf to them.

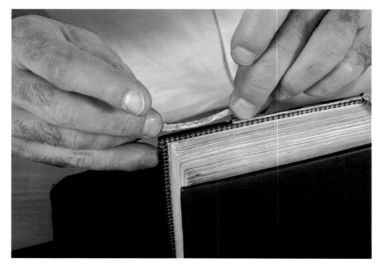

▲ **19.** Use the cotton to seat the gold completely on the surface.

▲**20.** Decorate the endcap with fillets and small hand stamps in the shape of stars or little pearls.

▲ **21.** Apply the roll to the edge of the cover. Tool the head and tail edges, followed by the fore edges, which should join the others at the corners.

▲ **22.** Clean the edge as before.

► **23.** Attach the end sheets after the tooling is finished.

Bas-Relief Onlays

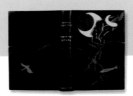

B *as-relief onlays are one of the most dramatic binding decorations. This decoration is often enhanced with other techniques such as gold tooling and gilding.*

To make a bas-relief onlay, you'll follow a drawn design. Then you'll lend volume and texture by using burins. This technique produces a much more dimensional effect than the simpler method of making a collage with various leather onlays.

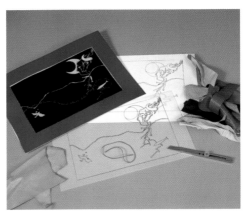

▲ **1.** Once the book has had its boards attached, take the exact measurements of the cover. Use a pencil to execute the rough draft of your design for the cover. Place lightweight tracing paper over it, and trace all the lines and shapes. The version of the design is known as the original. Once it's finished, make several photocopies that you can use as patterns for cutting out the leather onlays.

▲ **2.** To make the onlays, the leather must be very thinly pared. Place each piece on a board, and place the corresponding pattern on top of each color. Hold the paper and leather in place on the board with transparent tape in preparation for the final trimming.

▲ **3.** Trim them with a fine hobby knife or scalpel with a curved blade to avoid damaging the leather. As you cut out the onlays, they'll be released between the paper and the board, since there's no adhesive to hold them in place.

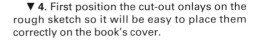

▼ **4.** First position the cut-out onlays on the rough sketch so it will be easy to place them correctly on the book's cover.

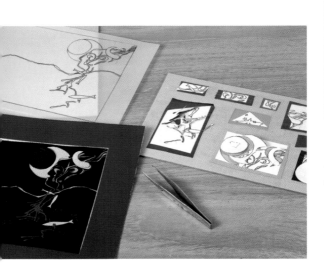

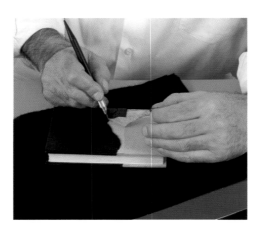

▲**5.** On this particular book, two pieces of leather were used to create the cover. We used the tracing paper pattern as a guide to cut out the first piece of leather to the exact size. Once this portion of the cover was covered with leather and dried, we used a hot burin to mark the pattern's edge.

▲ **6.** After you complete this part of the inlay process on any book, remove the tracing paper, and you'll see the mark that the burin has made on the leather. Use a hobby knife to trim the excess leather off along this mark. Do this carefully to avoid damaging the board. Follow the same procedure to cut, attach, and fit the second piece of leather next to the first.

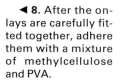

◄ **8.** After the onlays are carefully fitted together, adhere them with a mixture of methylcellulose and PVA.

▲ 7. Once the book is covered, use the original design as a guide to mark the various lines and shapes with the burin. Keep the burin at a constant temperature and give it a slight movement from the inside toward the outside of each shape to create the effect of volume. The more body the leather has, the more volume it will take on.

►**9.** Use a piece of cotton moistened with water to remove any leftover adhesive along the edges of the onlays, and allow the finished design to dry completely.

◄ **11.** On this particular book, the onlay decoration is supplemented with gold stamping and some stainless steel appliqués. This was done after the book was completely finished.

▲ 10. Once the whole project is dry, you'll still need to use the hot burin to set and define the onlay pieces on the leather. Don't press directly on top of them. Simply define the outline of the pieces to lend them volume and adhere them firmly to the cover.

► **12.** To protect and finish the leather, hold the book in a vertical position, and use an airbrush to apply a light layer of water-based lacquer to the surface. Apply a second coat as a final finish.

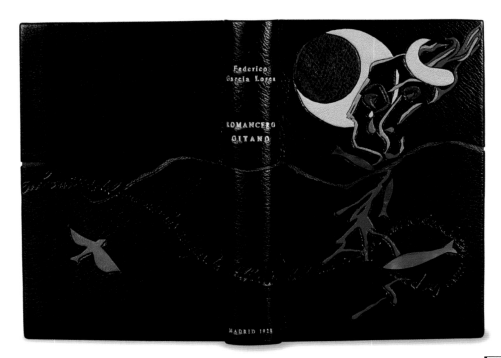

Gallery

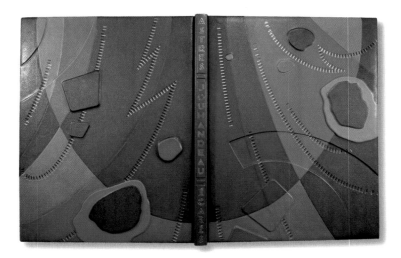

▲ Santiago Brugalla

▲ Josep Cambras

▲ Jordi de la Rica

▲ Manuel Bueno

▲ Germana Cavalcanti

▲ Ramón Gómez

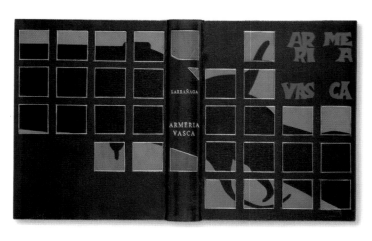

▲ Miquel Monedero

◄ Hermanos Galván

Acknowledgments

I must express thanks to Germana Cavalcanti and Pilar Estrada for the invaluable collaboration they contributed to the creation of this book.

To Ramon Serra for the contribution of knowledge in the section on the history of bookbinding

To Montse Buxó and Fernando de la Sierra for the sections on flyleaves and paper restoration, respectively

To Ferran Pujol, Georgina Aspa, Oriol Miró, and Jordi Cambras for their availability in the project

To Mariano Garcia y Conchita Aldonza for the many years of shared work

To the Education Department of the Council of Barcelona

To the professors of the Escola d'Arts i Oficis, especially Josep Asunción and Jordi Catafal, to whom I owe the contact with the publisher that made this book possible

To Parramón Publishing, and especially the editor Lluis Borràs, for his competence, his confidence, and his support at all times

To the photographer Jordi Vidal for his professionalism

To the photographer Marti Gasull for his selfless collaboration and support in this project

To Txema Pinto for years of collaboration on book designs

To the binders Emilio and Santiago Grugalla, Manuel Bueno, Ramón Gomez, Miquel Monedaro, and Jordi de la Rica, who in one war or another have formed my criteria and level as a bookbinder

To the clients, booksellers, and friends for the confidence and support shown through the years

To my wife Carme and my children Jordi and Marta for their unconditional support and for the patience they demonstrated at all times.

To my parents Gaspar and Maria Dolors, to whom I am indebted for finding myself immersed in this fascinating world of bookbinding, and who encouraged my development by providing me with the support I always needed.

Josep Cambras

Bibliography

Monje Ayala, Mariano. *El Arte de la Encuadernacón*. Labor Publishing, Barcelona, 1944.

Lenormand, Sebastian. *Nouveau Manuel Complet du Relieur*. Librairie Encyclopédique de Roret, Paris, 1840.

Johnson, Arthur. *Manual de Encuadernación*. Hermann Blume, Madrid, 1989.

Castañeda, Vicente. *Ensayo de un Diccionario Biográfico de Encuadernadores Españoles*. Maestre Publishing, Madrid, 1958.

Miquel i Planas, Ramon. *Bibliofilia*. Barcelona, 1911-1920.

Haldane, Duncane. *Islamic Bookbindings*. Penshurst Press Limited, England, 1983. Devaux, Ives. Deux Siècles de Reliure. Editions Pygmalion, Nancy, 1987.

Devaux, Ives. *Deux Siécles de Reliure*. Editions Pygmalion, Nancy, 1987.

Devaux, Ives. *Dorure et Décoration des Reliures*. Dessain and Tolra Publilshing, Paris 1980.

AA.VV. *Les Tranchefiles Brodées, Etude Historique et Technique*. Bibliothèque Nationale, Paris, 1980.

Kraemer Koeller, Gustavo. *Tratado de la Previsión del Papel y de la Conservación de Bibliotecas y Archivos*. General Office of Archives and Libraries, Madrid, 1973.

Middleton, Bernard. *The Restoration of Leather Bindings*. The British Library, London, 1998.

Doizy, Marie-Ange, Ipert, Stephane. *Le Papier Marbré*. Technorama Publishing, Argenton-sur-Creuse, 1985.

Index

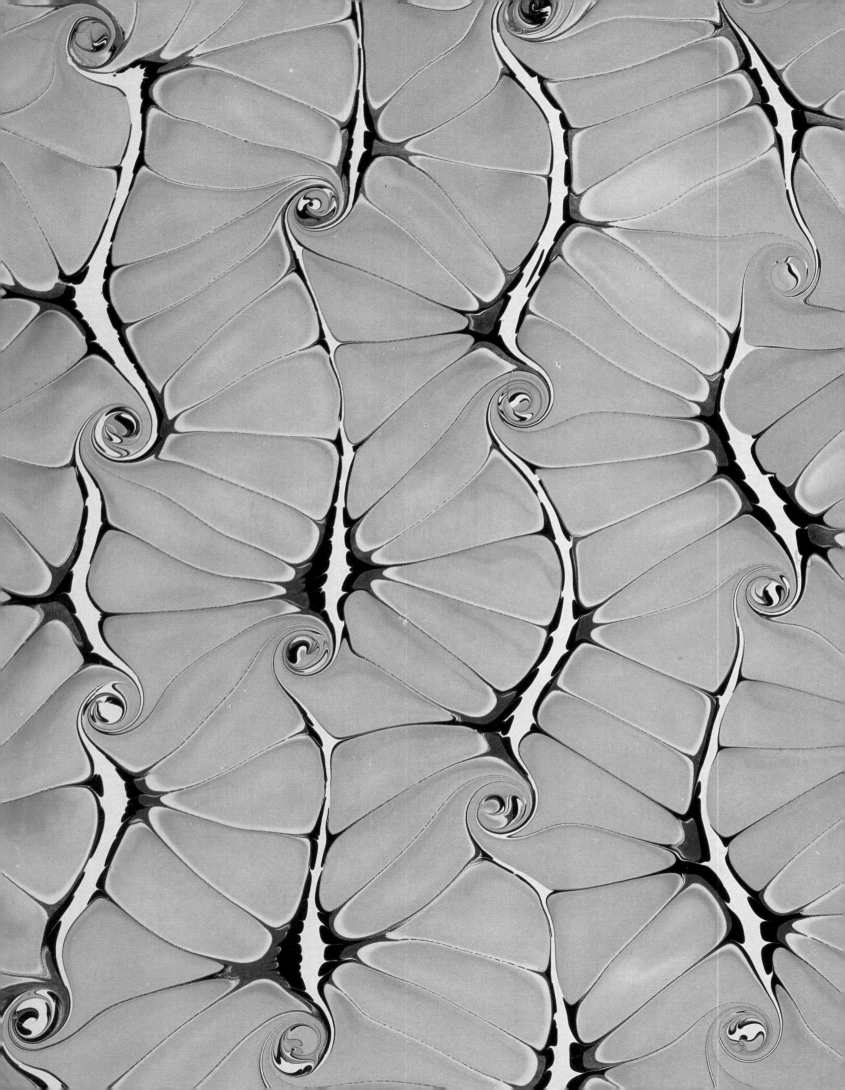